BRIAN COCKERILL
& LEE DUFFY
THE TAXMAN OF TEESSIDE

WRITTEN BY BRIAN AND EMMA COCKERILL WITH STEVE WRAITH

Mojo Risin'
Publishing Ltd

Published in 2020 by Mojo Risin' Publishing Ltd
www.mojorisinpublishing.com

Copyright © 2020 Brian Cockerill, Emma Cockerill, Steve Wraith
All rights reserved

The moral rights of the authors have been asserted

No part of this book may be reproduced or transmitted in any form or by any means without the prior written permission of both the copyright owner and the publisher
Unauthorised use of images within this book will result in legal action

British Library Cataloguing in Publication Data:
A catalogue record for this book is available from the British Library

ISBN-13:
978-1-9163867-6-1

Cover design
David Stanyer

Layout
Neil Jackson, Media Arts
www.media-arts.co.uk

Printed & bound by PrintGuy
Proudly published Up North

This book is dedicated to my friend Lee and his brother Lawrie.
Both taken too soon.

Preface

Over the years many books have been written about myself and Lee Duffy and all of them have been factually incorrect and written by people who were not born or living in the area when we were active. I want to start with a list I put together. There were a lot of similaraties between myself and Lee Duffy and I wanted to share these with you:

- Lee was bullied as a child. So was I.
- Lee lived 4 half miles from me but we never met.
- John Black, who was a top fighter from Middlesbrough taught Lee to box.
- When I was 22 I started working for John Black. He also taught me how to box.
- Lee excelled at boxing and was a top fighter at a young age.
- I started weight training at a young age, had phenomenal strength and became a top fighter at a young age.
- Lee had a tattoo on his right arm when he was 16 years of age.
- I had the same tattoo on the same arm at 16. The tattoo was a Red Devil with 'born to raise hell' written on it . Duke Webb was the tattooist and he did both tattoos.
- Lee became the youngest doorman in Middlesbrough. I became the youngest doorman in Redcar
- Lee was shot in the left foot and ended up on crutches whilst I was attacked in Tommy Harrison's house and ended up on crutches.
- Lee was the most wanted person by Cleveland police. So was I.
- We were both the same age.
- Lee was barred from drinking in Teesside so was I.

When I look back at some of the things on that list it is like reading about a different person. I have turned by life around for the better. I've found God. I have a beautiful wife. I count myself very lucky to be alive.

I would also like to thank the members of Lee's family who have allowed us to use their input. This book is a true account of what really happened in Teesside in 1991, when I met Lee until his tragic death.

Rest in peace mate.
Brian Cockerill October 2020

Chapter One: The Encounter

In the late eighties and early nineties I was living in Redcar and running the doors of local bars and clubs in Teesside. When I first started working on the doors I worked in 'Leo's' in Redcar every night. I worked sometimes three, or four nights a week and I was fighting every night that I worked. I always had to be on my toes. The men in those days had morals. Sometimes you would get people you had beaten coming back and saying I was drunk or, you punched me slyly which wasn't the case, but they wanted a straightener which was a one on one fight on a beach, or in a field or carpark, and I always obliged. There wasn't a lot of grasses in those days either. Nobody really made statements like they do now because you would be made an outcast if you did. I'm not looking through rose tinted glasses when I say they were the good old days.

One night me and my mate Kev Kilty had been over to Durham to visit one of my doormen. On the way back I asked Kev if he fancied a a parmo which is a Teesside delicacy. It's a chicken fillet, in breadcrumbs with bechamel sauce, covered in cheese. We headed to our favouite restaraunt which was situated on Millbank Terrace in Redcar. We always went there as the food was really good. After our food we decided to nip over to Station Road to see a friend of ours, Jimmy Stubbs. It was a short walking distance from where we had just eaten. Just then a car came slowly by and turned onto Station Road. Kevin said it was Lee Duffy and John Fail. I'd never met either of them before. I had heard of Duffy though. I was a friend of John Black and worked for him and he told me that Lee was due out of jail. He vouched for him and said that he was a good lad and thought that we would get on and said that he would introduce us but that never happened.

They pulled up in the car right outside Jimmy's. Quick as a flash Kevin said "Let's give that a miss" and we decided to call and see Jimmy another time. As we turned back round to go back to the car I heard a voice shouting "Oi Oi" so I turned round and there was Lee Duffy, walking towards me in what seemed like a friendly manner. "Whats your name mate?" he said.

Looking back I was too gullible, and not too streetwise, and I just stood there expecting to shake his hand. John Fail was now out of the car and had also started walking forward and he was drinking from a bottle of lager, which he kept switching from hand to hand. I turned my head to look at him and took my eyes off Lee. I was standing square on and out of nowhere Lee hit me with a left hook on the sly. Something I later found out that he was known for. He had taken me by surprise. I remember just seeing a flash and I dropped instantly, but not fully and I managed to push myself straight back up. I was shaken but had managed to recover quickly. Lee then started running at me and grabbed my legs, rugby tackling me. This was his first mistake.

At the time my legs were massive, they were 36 inches in circumference and I weighed nearly 24 stones at the time. As he grabbed at my legs I split my legs apart and grabbed him by the jumper, lifting him off his feet before running him into a wall. Lee weighed about 15 stone and he tried to push me back but had no chance with my strength. I held him with my left hand, as a few nights before I had broken my middle finger on my right hand in another altercation. I managed to head butt him twice which I could see had really hurt him. He was on his back so I jumped on him and kneed him in the face twice and then elbowed him in the face. I was just about to bite him when Lee shouted to his pal John to get me off him. There was no way John Fail could handle me so he hit me over the head with the bottle. Lucky for me It didn't smash. I turned on Faily and swatted him away like a fly and then turned my attentions back to Duffy. Kev was keeping an eye out for the bizzies and shouting "One on one lads." Duffy was still stunned and on the floor. I decided to leave it. I knew I couldn't continue fighting two people with a broken finger and I had nothing more to prove. I headed towards my mate Mick Stores house over the road to pull myself together and take in what had just happened. Mick was another doorman and a good friend who is sadly no longer with us.

By now Duffy had regained his composure and was walking towards me to have another go. John Fail was on the other side of the road shouting and bawling, telling Lee to drop me again and that he could beat me. Duffy was jumping about from side to side so as he got close to me I threw a massive left hook and then crouched down anticipating a return punch. I just missed Duffy by half an inch. He was using his brain and had kept out of my range. We could both box and we started weighing each other up. He came at me again so I grabbed a plastic bollard that was sticking out of the ground and I ran at him, hitting him with it. The bollard hit his hands and he jumped back and I could see fear in his eyes as he started to back off. I told him to call John Black to organise a straightener because I couldn't continue to fight them both with a broken hand.

A large crowd had now gathered. Duffy and Fail were heading back to their car but Duffy never took his eyes off me. "I've just dropped you" he shouted. "Yes, but with a sly punch and it didn't stop me getting back up and beating you" I said. As I got to Mick's front door he had appeared with a baseball bat but Duffy and Fail had got back into their car and driven off. As I was explaining what had happened to Mick, Kev appeared in his car. "You beat him there Brian, he was screaming like a pig on the floor." He was right. I had no marks or injuries at all. I just needed to give my hand time to heal and then put an end to the this situation once and for all.

Chapter Two: Training For The Fight

The next fight with Duffy would be a straightener. No sly punching. No mates there hitting me with bottles. This would be a proper fight and I knew I was going to win it because I was too strong for him. Deep down I think he knew that as well after our first encounter.

Everybody in Teesside was talking about the fight so I asked John Black to arrange it. However, the fight had put John in a tricky situation. He was friends with both me and Lee and said that he didn't want to get involved. We would need someone else to mediate and arrange the fight once my hand was healed. I decided to move in and train with Frankie Atherton in Redcar.

Frankie was a boxer who had fought at Madison Square Garden, in New York. He was an ABA champion and had then turned pro. He was around the same age with the same kind of character as Mickey, played by Burgess Meredith in the Rocky films. He was a great man and he introduced me to my wife Emma all those years ago. He had two labradors called Sam and Max and me and Frank would take them to the beach where I would do sprints. I had decided to drop down a weight so that my hand speed would be a lot faster and my fitness would be better. I'd also started running at 5am and was doing 5 mile runs.

One night the police stopped me and asked what I was running from. I told them I wasn't running from anyone but that I was training for a fight. They replied "Another one with Duffy?" I nodded and started running again. Even the police knew!

I had a piece of string tied to my washing line and would spend hours throwing combinations at it. I found it difficult to shadow box and this was an old method that John Black used, which I found easier. I was training hard and getting results. I was also at the gym each day, as well as boxing and running. I was the fittest I had ever been.

I was still working the doors at night. I would see people I knew from Southbank and Grangetown who had heard Duffy speaking about the first fight. He had told people that I had 'hideous strength' and that he couldn't understand why he had never heard of me before. He had bumped into a good friend of mine, Bryan Flartey and explained that he had fought 'Scotch Brian' and was getting ready for a rematch. I was known to some as 'Scotch' because I was born in Scotland. Bryan had told him that I had been training hard and that he was going to have his work cut out. He wasn't wrong. Hearing all of these comments and stories gave me a great deal of confidence. I had also heard a story that Duffy had been dropped by a lad I knew called Mark Johnson, who was a lot lighter than me, in the Kings Head in Grangetown during a fight. There was no doubt in my mind that I was going to win this fight. He was clearly vulnerable.

My hand was now healed so I started to use the punch bag and spar with people which brought my speed on and my power. I was fit, confident and ready to go. I got in touch with Mark Johnson and another pal called Addish and told them that I was ready to fight Duffy. I didn't drive and would need them to pick me up so I could go and look for Lee. They agreed.

We went to all his known haunts that day but there was no sign of him so I tried again the following night with another mate of mine called Nipper. We were driving round Eston when we suddenly saw him pass us going in the opposite direction in a Ford Sierra. Both cars screeched to a halt. He saw me and I could see him beckoning me over with his hands. I got out of the car and took my top off. I was wearing a blue vest, tracksuit bottoms and a pair of army boots. I heard Mark shout "Go on Bri." He was up for a fight as well. I was focussed. This was going to be quick.

I ran towards the car. Duffy shook his driver Craig Howard's shoulder and the car started. I knew Craig from a gym we both used to train at. They were trying to drive off so I jumped on the back of the car causing it to stall. I then ran to the passenger side and tried to open the door but it was locked. I could hear Duffy shouting "Go…Go…" to Craig. He managed to get the car started and they drove off leaving me angry and frustrated. Mark was on the phone to Kevin Kilty telling him what had just happened. We decided not to follow them. He clearly didn't want to fight me. We headed to Redcar and I met up with Emma. A lovely girl that I had started seeing a bit of, in between training and working. "Have you just chased Lee Duffy?" she asked. I told her I had. I laughed at how quickly news had spread. It felt like a victory without even throwing a punch, but I still wanted my day on the street with him to set the record straight once and for all.

A few days after this incident I was due in court. As I was walking towards the court I saw Duffy drive past me in a green Mondeo wearing a pair of sunglasses. It is the car he is sitting on in that infamous photo of him in his shorts. He was on his own. As he approached me he began to slow down and he pointed his fingers like a gun at me saying that he was going to shoot me. My anger hadn't subsided. I went balistic and I started running towards his car shouting "Fight me you shithouse." As I got near him he drove off again. There was no doubt in my mind that he was scared to fight me. He'd had two good opportunities to get things sorted but on both occasions had chosen to drive away. I went into the courts, where a few of my doormen were meeting me. "Duffys just left. He's due back up at 2pm with another lad," said one of my mates. I told them what had just happened and that I wanted to get it sorted there and then. My case got adjourned so I decided to wait outside the courts till Duffy returned. As I was waiting a solicitor came past me called Bernie Tomlin and asked me why I was waiting outside with my lads. I told him I was waiting for Duffy. His eyes lit up. "Oh I can't wait to see this," he said. It seemed everybody wanted this fight to take place except Duffy, because as time passed it became clear that having seen me there he had no intention of coming back.

The following weekend I was at 'Manhattans nightclub 'in Redcar. With Mick who had been there on the day of the first fight. He wanted to introduce me to Peter Hoe, who was a top boxer from Eston. I had heard a lot about him and was only too happy to be introduced. Peter and his family had also had trouble with Duffy in the past and had offered to fight Lee at Conker Wood near Eston hills over a dispute they had. Duffy rang Peter and said "I don't want to fight you, you're my friend" so he ended up meeting Peter and shaking his hand to put an end to the matter. Sometime before this incident Peter's older brother Tom who was another top fighter had been slyed by Duffy. Sound familiar? Tom seen him not long after and put it on Duffy's toes. They fought, with Tom Hoe coming out on top after a long, tough battle. Duffy shook hands with Tom and they went their separate ways.

    Peter and I hit it off instantly and agreed to keep in touch then out of the blue he said 'Can I ask you a favour?" I told him to name it. He asked me if I could leave the fight with Duffy for a bit as Lee had been shot in the foot in the 'blues.' The blues were houses in the 'Boro that the Jamaican lads used to run. They were underground, after-hours clubs where you could get a drink and whatever else you fancied. I was quite taken aback and explained to Peter what had happened at that first fight and that I had been sly punched and then hit with a bottle. Peter listened intently. He was an old school fighter and believed in a fair fight. He was the type of person that would have a straightener with you and then win or lose he would shake your hand afterwards and buy you a drink. He seemed genuinely shocked and taken aback at what I had to tell him. "Well if that is what happened Brian then I do not blame you for not leaving it." he said.

    Duffy was starting to try my patience. I just wanted to fight Lee Duffy and put an end to the matter. As for Peter he was one of the most genuine lads I've ever had the pleasure to meet and we formed a strong bond that night. Sadly Peter was later murdered in his own home after being stabbed to death by two scumbags with knives.

Chapter Three: Cat and Mouse

This game of cat and mouse was doing my head in. Ozzie Bingham another friend of mine from Whinney Banks seemed to have more luck seeing Duffy than me over the next few weeks. Ozzie had been at a lock-in at 'Rumours Nightclub,' in 'Boro. Duffy had turned up and sat at the table with Ozzie and several doormen that worked there. Naturally the conversation turned to fights and fighting and Lee was asked about the hardest fight that he had ever had. He said it was against a man called 'Scotch Brian,' who just wouldn't go down. Ozzie didn't know that Lee was actually talking about me. It was becoming clear to me now that this fight was never going to happen, but I still needed to stay fit just in case and have my wits about me.

Ozzie already knew Lee prior to this though. Ozzie had been working at a pub in 'Boro called 'Touch Down'. He was ejecting two lads from the bar with the owner Paul Barber. The two lads had been messing about and pouring beer over each other. Duffy was sat in the bar with a lad called Peter Sugget. Suddenly Lee jumped off the chair he was sitting in and said to Ozzie, "Don't put them out like that put them out like this." Lee then hit one of the lads who went straight down on the floor. He'd knocked him out. Ozzie and Paul had to pick him up and put him outside. Within forty minutes there were roughly forty people at the bar wanting to fight Duffy. They were all from different housing estates such as Brambles Farm, Thorntree and Palister Park but were all part of the football hooligan firm at the time and had all been drinking in the 'Albert Pub' when Duffy had taken a liberty with one of their mates. The lad that had been knocked out was the bar manager's son. Seeing the baying mob outside and realising it was for him Duffy ran out the back door and scarpered and it was left to Ozzie, Paul, along with the Jeffery's brothers Molly and Brian and another lad called John Cullan to sort the hooligans out.

Sometime later he saw Lee again at the blues in Kensington Road in Middlesbrough. Lee had wanted to take the barmaid out who worked in 'Chaplin's pub', but she wouldn't go out with him. This particular night she had gone to the blues with Ozzie. They had been in the blues about half an hour, and Ozzie had started knocking a joint up. You had to go in the back passage in the blues where there was a bit of light to make the joint so he had left the barmaid to fend for herself. Two minutes later she was in front of him but she was soaking wet. Duffy had arrived and had seen them together so he had grabbed a drink and thrown it over her. He then turned to Ozzie and pushed him over. Ozzie knew better than to get straight up so he stayed down on the floor.

The owner of the blues, Ramsey, had seen the commotion and he jumped over the counter with an axe and told Duffy to get out. Duffy didn't argue but he promised Ramsey he would be back. He didn't keep his promise. A few nights later Ozzie saw him in the old 'Empire' sitting in the corner. He was quite subdued with his foot up on a stool. It turned out that he had been shot in the foot. Ozzie was with his mates Alan Rogers and 'Shandy Boyce' and he told them that he felt uncomfortable and wanted to leave but they weren't having it. Ozzie needn't have worried. Lee didn't even notice him. He clearly had other issues on his mind.

Chapter Four: Shotgun Showdown

I had a call from Mick in Redcar. Something had happened with Duffy and he wanted to see me. When I arrived there was a few other lads there including Paul Bryan and Dave Williams. We all had one thing in common. We had all had trouble with Lee Duffy or Lee Harrison. The lads started telling me that they had just been at a garage in the Longlands area of Middlesbrough and had just sawed down a shotgun to go looking for Duffy but as they were doing this Lee Duffy and Lee Harrison had pulled into the garage. There were five people at the garage that afternoon including a bodybuilder from Redcar. Lee Duffy made a beeline straight for him and asked him if he was with the others and looking for him. The lad said "No mate, I'm here to buy a car!" At that point Dave had appeared with the shotgun and started screaming and shouting at Lee that he was going to shoot him. The bodybuilder didn't hang around whilst Duffy remained calm and replied "Come on then, do it. Sack all that shouting and them veins popping out your face just do it. You can't miss can you?" Dave was still shouting "I will do it, I will do it ". But Dave couldn't do it. He didn't have it in him. The five of them jumped in a car and sped off back to Redcar. The reality of the situation began to sink in with Dave after the event and he admitted that he had been surprised that Duffy and Harrison had fronted them up. They were team handed and tooled up yet somehow Duffy had ended up putting it on their toes.

Dave told me that I had to fight him to put all this trouble to bed, and that he would pay me to do it. I told him not to be stupid. I didn't want his money. I just needed a driver to help me find him as I still hadn't passed my test and didn't have a license. He gave me the number of lad called Glenn and said that he would happily drive me around to get this sorted once and for all. I rang Glenn the next day and he picked me up in a Fiesta. We ran about all over 'Boro looking for him but we had no joy. We even headed over to Lee's brother in law Terry Stockells. I went up to the door alone and asked him if Duffy was there but Terry said he wasn't. I asked Terry to tell him that I was looking for him and he said he would. When I headed back to the car Glenn was not in the driver's seat. In fact he was nowhere to be seen. He was hiding in the bushes with a handgun. When I saw him I asked him, "What the fuck you doing with that?" He told me that the people who got him to run me about had said shoot Duffy if Brian wins, loses, or draws! I couldn't believe what I was hearing but that wasn't all. When we got back in the car he told me to look under my seat. There were two more handguns under it and he explained that in the boot was the shotgun Dave had threatened Lee with at the garage in Longlands. I was furious. I have always fought fairly. Guns are not my thing. I told Glenn to fuck off. I didn't want to see him again. He didn't need telling twice.

It was about a year later that he resurfaced in a nightclub that I was looking after and he was selling E's (ecstasy) so I levelled him and broke his jaw. If I am honest it was more about the incident with the guns and the fact that if he had shot somebody that night then we both could have been lifed off. He eventually moved down South, away from the area for good.

I needed somebody else to drive me and Paul Cook volunteered his services. I decided to head over to Grangetown where some of his mates lived but again I drew a blank. At least Paul was waiting in the car for me when I came back and with not a gun in sight. At another house one of Duffy's mates girlfriends came to the window. "No, I haven't seen him" she said. "Well tell him Brian Cockerill is looking for him," I said as I got back into the motor.

Tony Stubbs was another close friend who stepped up to the plate to chauffeur me around. We had worked the door together for many years and I could trust him not to let me down if it all came on top. Tony was from the same area as Lee, so he knew everywhere Lee went so one day we decided to start at 'Southbank Pool Hall' and crack on until we found him. From there we went into the 'Commercial Pub' where my pal Derek Beattie was sitting in the corner. He knew we were looking for Duffy and he said that he had not been in. We told people in there that we were looking for Lee and that if they saw him to tell him that we had been in. From there we headed to the 'Princess Alice' but again we drew a blank. It was obvious that he had gone to ground and was avoiding a lot of his regular haunts. From the 'Alice' we headed into Middlesbrough to the 'blues' and yes, you've guessed it, he hadn't been there either so after a stop off in Grangetown to see a mutual friend, Tony Johns, we headed home.

Every year the fair would come to Eston. This particular year Lee had broken cover and was on the dodgems with his girlfriend. As you, the reader will know, fairgrounds are run by travellers and the man who ran this ride was unaware of who Lee was. As the ride finished Lee stayed on to have another go and the man told him in a rather cheeky manner to "get off." Lee got up out of the car and he wasn't impressed. "Do you know who I am?" The traveller couldn't care less and he squared up to Lee who decked him with one punch. Another four lads had arrived to back up the traveller and three of them suffered a similar fate as the fifth ran off to get help. Lee wasn't hanging around. He had proved his point.

The man who owned the fair approached a friend of mine called John. We went to meet the owner at the Cross Keys in Guisborough and he asked me how much it would be to sort the trouble out and stop Lee from going there and causing trouble. The man said he didn't want his name mentioned or any come backs. I told him that I would do it for two grand. We shook hands and he agreed to pay me when it was done. Now I just had to find him.

But before I could, word reached me that Lee had been shot outside a 'blues' club. Nothing to do with me of course, but with John's help we spoke to the fair owner and told him we'd sorted out his little problem. The traveller was happy to pay up. It was by far the easiest money I've ever made!

A few nights later I was out with 'Gunner' from Eston and we had decided to go to Middlesbrough. We'd seen our mate Gary Russell, and went to a club called 'Wickers World.' Paul and Mark Debrick had the door there and they were quick to tell me that I had just missed Duffy. He had been in an hour earlier. Bingo!

We were on I thought, but my joy turned to disappointment as nobody knew where he had gone. He had been causing trouble and had hit one of the door lads, Peter Wilson, on the back of the neck with a can of 'redstripe.' He ended up in hospital with a broken neck. It was pointless looking for him. He would have gone to ground again as the police had been called and he would have known that they were looking for him.

The next day I decided to call in to North Tees Hospital to visit Peter Wilson with another lad, 'Cookie.' I didn't know Wilson personally but I just wanted to give him a lift and let him know he had back up. It costs nothing to be nice in this world. We got shown to the ward and he was laid there with a metal cage around his neck. I felt so sorry for him. He was pleased to see us. Before we left I gave him one of my business cards and told him to call me if he had any more issues. When I got home later that day my phone rang. Lee Duffy had been arrested.

Chapter Five: Double Trouble

Duffy was remanded and I was sick as fuck. With Duffy behind bars any hope of a second fight was put on hold. I was back on the doors and if I am honest feeling sick and deflated. I just wanted to fight Duffy and move on. One of the big issues with door work is the time it gives you to think. I needed something else in my life to keep me occupied other than training and slinging out pissed punters. Mark Miller was from the same area as Duffy, Southbank, and he came to me with a proposal. With Duffy locked up he had started 'taxing' the local dealers. By 'taxing' I mean taking the dealers drugs, money, cars and whatever else they had of value off them. It was easy money, and it wasn't as if they were going to go running to the police now was it? Mark knew most of the dealers on his doorstep so he would pick the targets and we would go along together. It gave me a bit of a buzz, relieved the bore- dom and gave me a lot more cash.

We had a good run for the first few weeks and things were going well. The Duffy situation was firmly in the back of my mind until I got a call to say that he had been given Judge in chambers and was going to be released.
On the day of his release me and Mark were sitting in 'The Kings Head' pub which was run by a man called Trevor Fairwell. The phone rang in the bar and something instinctively told me that it was Duffy ringing for me. I was right. I put it straight on him. " Hello Lee. When are we going to get this sorted? I'll fight you anywhere just tell me where and when." I waited for a cocky response and a time and place but what he said surprised me. "Look Brian It's 'nowt to do with fighting. I just want to apologise and shake your hand." I could not believe what I was hearing. He continued. "It wasn't me that day, it was Faily winding me up. He kept saying look at the size of him and do you think you could beat him. I just wasn't thinking." This seemed too good to be true and I didn't believe a word he was saying. He finished, "Look I'm at me Mams will you come round?" I took a sharp intake of breath, I was still taking this all in. "Yes ok, but you better not be setting me up," I said. "I'm not, I'll see you soon Brian." He put the phone down. I told Mark what had just happened and he agreed to give me a lift over.

All kinds of thoughts were going through my mind as we travelled the short distance to his Mam's house. When we arrived I got out of the car with Mark. I got to the door and before I had time to knock Lee's girlfriend answered and invited me in. Lee's Mam was in the kitchen. "He's in there" she said. I walked into the living room and Lee was on the settee tying his laces. He looked up at me and said, "Look at the size of you, I must have been mad!" He stood up and shook my hand and apologised. I looked at him and knew it was sincere. Just then one of his mates appeared behind me. "I thought you two were fighting?" Lee turned to him and said "No mate. I've just apologised." He then looked at me again and said, "You've got some bottle like… coming here… I wouldn't have come to yours alone."

I smiled. I felt more relaxed as it was clear now that Lee had no ulterior motives. He was keen for me to clear the air with John Fail too, the lad who had wound Lee up and who had hit me with a bottle of lager. I agreed. It made sense. Then we all jumped in Mark's motor to head over to Middlesbrough to see Fail.

Lee was always full of mischief and he said, "When we get there wind him up a bit. Offer him out!" I agreed, it would be good to see the panic on his face after the liberty he had taken with me that day. Once we arrived Lee went into the house and said, "You've got a problem John." His face dropped and he said, "Why, what have I done Lee?" Lee carried on, "Now't to do with me Faily. Me and Brian have shook hands, but he's out there now and wants to see you. You're on your own with this one." As Lee is saying this I am outside his door shouting and bawling and telling him to get outside and that I wanted a straightener. John was whiter than Casper The Ghost as he came to the door. "I ..I… can't fight you Brian.." he said. We let it go for a few more seconds before we all burst out laughing. The relief on John's face was clear for all to see. I walked towards him and we shook hands. The war was over.

We went inside and Lee started to explain that Craig Howard had been writing and visiting him in jail and had been telling him about me and Mark 'taxing' the local dealers and that we had been taking it to another level. He had also spoken highly of me, as had others in jail and said that he should look at putting things right and teaming up. "Brian is as strong as an Ox and has a lot of bottle," said Craig. Lee was keen on forming a partnership. "Look we are the best fighters around here. If we team up then who's going to stop us?" He was right.

Not only was Lee an extremely good fighter but it was apparent that he was streetwise and intelligent. He also had what you could call a sixth sense. He explained that in those days I had been looking for him that he always seemed to know when I was coming and had a few near misses. I wanted to know why when he saw me in his car he would slow down and mock me and then drive away. He explained that he was playing mind games and that he knew that I would always be on edge waiting to see if he was in the next car that I saw. He recalled a time when he knew I was in a house that he had pulled up outside of. He was of course right. I had sent out a young lad to taunt him and say, "Come on then I'll fight you." Lee had laughed and driven away. " I knew you were in that house Brian because there is no way that kid would have been so brave, not in a million years." As I said, Lee was streetwise and intelligent. The partnership to me seemed like a good idea and we felt that there was no time like the present. So myself, Lee and a couple of other lads went to Redcar to do our first 'tax' together.

We tracked down a dealer that we knew and we grabbed him and bundled him into a car. We took him to the Gare in Redcar just by the lighthouse and we tied him up with a strong rope around his legs and put a bag over his head. We asked him where his money and his stash was but he wouldn't tell us anything. So growing impatient with him I picked him up and threw him in the sea. He must have been petrified, not to mention freezing cold. Whilst in the sea this young dealer came to his senses and decided that he could remember what we wanted to know and that he wanted to tell us everything. So I dragged him out of the North Sea and bundled him back into the motor. He directed us to a bed and breakfast on Station Road. He went in on his own, his shoes squelching. Moments later he came back out with a grand, which we shared between the three of us. We got £300 a piece and bunged Lee's driver £100. It was a good start for the partnership and not bad for a mornings work.

    I was hungry and suggested we go to 'Roy's café', in Middlesbrough for some food. As we walked up to the counter there were a few shocked faces to see me and Lee together. We told them that we had teamed up and were now partners. Everyone agreed it was a good move. After a bit of food and a cuppa we came out of the cafe to the carpark to see the car had been clamped. The man who had clamped the car was still in the carpark. Lee said to him to him, "Who the fuck are you? Do you know who I am? If you don't get that clamp off I will get him to rip it off" and he pointed at me. Looking back now the man was just doing his job but his face was white as a sheet as he ran over to the car and started fumbling for his key to take the clamp off. He was quite literally shaking so I tapped him on the shoulder and said, "Don't worry mate." It seemed to calm him down. I shook his hand and he thanked me for putting him at ease. From there we drove to the pool hall in Southbank next to the 'Commercial pub.'

    As we walked in there was about thirty kids between the age of twelve and fifteen and they all stopped playing pool and doing what they were doing and all came over to say hello to Lee. It was like the scene from Oliver Twist when they see Fagin return. Lee was really good to the kids and it was clear they looked up to him like a God. He was always giving them change from his pocket. On one occasion one of the kids didn't have a coat on whilst all the others did. Lee said to him, "Where's your coat son?" The lad told him that he didn't have one. So Lee took off his coat and gave it to him. The lad was over the moon, I can still picture his face now. It was then that I realised that there was another side to Lee Duffy. A kind hearted, caring side.

    We left the snooker hall early afternoon and went to fill the car up at a garage on the way to 'Boro to do another 'tax.' I filled the car up and I went to pay at the cashiers desk. Lee's mate followed me in as I was paying and asked me if I wanted any chocolate or snacks. I told him I was okay for now and I paid the girl behind the counter. After we'd both got back in the car Lee asked his mate to pass him some chocolate. His mate handed him about twenty bars of assorted sweets and it was then that I noticed his pockets were stuffed full. This became a regular occurrence when we were working together and it used to drive me mad. I wouldn't have been able to stand the embarrassment of having my name in the 'Evening Gazette' for shoplifting! "Don't worry 'Big Fella' he won't get caught" Lee would say with a broad smile on his face.

We drew a blank for the rest of the day looking for dealers to 'tax' but, we had put our differences aside once and for all and formed a formidable team. As Lee and the lads dropped me off at home Lee shouted "I'll call for you in the morning Brian" I nodded and laughed as he drove off. We were like two kids arranging to play out the next day, but I was looking forward to it. I was in a much happier place.

Craig Howard had trained for most of his life and had entered 'Mister Universe' competitions. He'd come sixth in 'Mr England'. He looked like one of those bodybuilders you would see on a Californian beach. It was Craig that had got Lee Duffy onto steroids after our fight. With the steroids and training he did with Craig he put two and a half stone on. Lee said to me one night that in the first fight I had thrown him about with ease so he thought if he gained weight and muscle that he would have more of a chance of beating me if we ended up scrapping on the floor. I started laughing as he was telling me this and he asked me what was so funny. I told him that I had decided to drop two stone for the next fight so that I would me more agile, so Lee started laughing. Craig had been listening to our conversation and compared us to Napoleon and the Duke Of Wellington going into battle and working on our strategies and plans. We all burst out laughing again. Lee also admitted that another part of his game plan was to get me on a 'heavy leg day'. What he meant by that was that after squatting when you train legs heavy like I was and pushing yourself to the limit, you come out drained and exhausted and your legs are like bambi on ice because your legs are full of blood and you can hardly walk. I must admit I was shocked at how much thought Lee had put into his planning. Lee was keen to know if I had a plan to catch him off guard. I told him I did and that I was hoping to catch him in a pub or club so he couldn't jump around. After hearing that Lee turned to Craig and said, "I told you he was smart didn't I?" Lee then looked at me, and said, "I'm glad that we didn't fight though Big Fella."

Chapter Six: Taxing, Training and Tantrums

The next day a top of the range BMW pulled up outside of my house. It was Lee and Craig Howard was driving. Craig had his window open and shouted "Now then, now then" as I walked out towards the car. It was a saying that Lee would adopt and has become so well known for. We were heading to Darlington first. Lee had some issues over there with a couple of lads and wanted to sort it out. We got there in no time and went to a Garage where we found the two lads. After a very brief discussion we took a Ford Granada off them. It turned out that the lads owed Craig £500 for coke. The car itself was worth £3000. It was in good nick and we managed to sell it for £2000. Me and Lee got £750 each and we gave Craig the £500 he was owed. I was going to share it three ways but Lee reminded me that Craig was only owed £500 and that if it hadn't been for me and Lee then he would not have got it back. Looking at it that way I had to agree. Like I said earlier. Lee was bright and always on the ball when it came to money. "We always get the lions share Big Fella," he would say.

After a good result in Darlington we headed over to Stockton to go and train at 'Moore's Gym' that was run by Paul Epstein. I had never seen Lee train so I was interested to see him in action. He started showing off with a 308 lbs on a bench press which he really struggled with, only managing to get one rep. I got on the bench after him and did 22 controlled reps. Lee was shocked at how strong I was. "I've just seen it, but I don't believe it . You've got alien strength," Lee said. As we continued to train I was aware of a nervousness in the gym from other people. A few people were walking out before they had finished training. It's not something I had ever noticed before. Clearly the sight of me and Lee together had not quite sunk in with everybody. Having seen me bench, Lee was keen to know what my best squat was.
Paul answered for me. "I've seen him do 803 lb squat for three reps, a 630 lb bench press and a 2000 lb leg press." Lee shook his head in disbelief. It was clear that he was trying to find a chink in my training armour and something that he could do better than me. He started doing one-legged squats and asked me if I could do them. I was too big for this exercise but Lee had good balance and found them easy. He was happy at last.

The next day Craig turned up on his own, there was no sign of Lee. We headed down to Darlington in separate cars but this time to train. I had passed my test now so had a bit of freedom. Craig was doing some good business in 'Darlo' with the coke and liked to head over there in case there were any issues. After a good training session we headed to a wine bar that Craig frequented but a couple of doorman tried to stop us going in as we had our tracksuits on. I took one look at them and ended up knocking both of them out. We didn't want to hang around so went for some food instead and then back to Craig's house. I went in his for a cuppa and met his girlfriend Nicky. She was a bodybuilder like Craig and we sat talking about steroids, growth hormone and training amongst other things. As I was leaving Craig said that he would pick me up the next day to go training again. I jumped in my car and headed home.

The next day Craig rang me early and asked if I minded driving to his house to meet him as he had a little job for me. I told him I would be over as quick as I could. I got myself ready and then I drove over in a blue Hyundai car, which I had 'taxed' off a lad in 'Boro a few weeks earlier. I parked up in Craig's street and knocked on his door. Craig explained that he was owed some money in Redcar and he wanted my help to get it back. I agreed so we got in his car and made our way over. We went to two houses to pick a few quid up and all I had to do was sit in the passenger seat. He ended up giving me £200 quid for doing nothing! Craig knew I was a face in Redcar and that's why he wanted to be seen with me when he went to pick up the debts. It made sense to me and got me an earner so I was happy.

We drove back to Craig's to get my car but when we pulled up I could see that the windscreen had been put through. As I got out to survey the damage Craig said, "Duffy's done that." I didn't understand. Why would our partner smash my windscreen? Craig then explained that Duffy could get jealous very easily and that despite him being off the radar for a few days he would not have liked the fact that me and Craig had been working and training together without him. I shook my head in disbelief. No way would Lee do that, I mean it was just childish. Craig insisted on getting my windscreen replaced which was kind of him.

The following day Lee resurfaced and I asked him "Why did you do it? I thought we were mates." He replied "We are mates, I just got a bit jealous as you'd gone off with Craig for a few days." I said "Is that it?" and we both started laughing about it. I realised how much Lee liked being with me. Even though it was childish I understood that to him it was a bit like 'Brian's my friend, not yours' and that was just Lee. To be fair to him he admitted it straight away and apologised. It turned out Craig was right all along. Because of his honesty and the fact that Craig had got it fixed for me I gave Lee a cuddle and laughed it off. It just wasn't worth falling out over.

That day Lee told me about the shootings prior to us teaming up. He said he'd been in the 'blues' and some lads from out of town were there. One of them reached under his coat whilst making a bee-line for Duffy. With so many people being in a small space the lad couldn't just pull the gun straight out and point it at Lee. So the lads were like sneaking over towards him. Lee was on the ball and saw the shotgun coming from the lads coat. So he grabbed the gun and it went off as he wrestled with it, hitting Lee in the foot. The lads scarpered while he managed to hobble outside and away from the 'blues.' He ended up near 'Scorpio's Tattooist' and managed to phone for an ambulance. The paramedics arrived and had found Lee bleeding in the doorway and took him straight to hospital. I asked Lee if it hurt when he got shot. He said, "Of course it fucking did you mad bastard, it nearly blew me fucking foot off and It burns like you couldn't imagine." He told me that it still gave him a lot of pain and sometimes when we were out we would have to stop the car so Lee could stretch his legs. It was the reason he smoked a lot of joints, to numb the pain.

Lee also told me the story of how another shooting had happened. He had gone to a house to 'tax' a lad and when he was in the house he gave the lad a slap so the lad handed over five thousand acid tabs. Lee had missed ten kilos of gear under a carpet and he was fuming when he found that out. Anyway the lad worked for a really well known dealer and he paid some lads to shoot Lee. On the night in question he was outside the blues talking when out of the corner of one eye he noticed a lad getting out of a car. The lad shouted "Duffy!" Lee turned towards him and the lad fired the gun. Lee said he saw a flash and then heard the bang. Lee said he jumped up in the air so most of the pellets went under him and missed and then the lad ran off. The pellets that actually grazed Lee were like salt grains. The type you would shoot pigeons with. Lee looked at me and said, "I can't believe you haven't been shot Big Fella, the way you're kicking doors in and 'taxing 'people." That certainly made me think.

Lee and I spent the next day in Middlesbrough finally ending up in the 'Havana nightclub' where I was introduced to a chirpy little guy who looked like Norman Wisdom, with the same mannerisms called Terry 'Dicko'. He was sawing a piece of wood as I met him. It turned out that he worked there and was doing odd jobs in the place for the owner. I also met another lad who was testing the microphones in the DJ Box called Lee Harrison, who was at that time a known football hooligan. Lee smiled when he saw me and Lee together and said, "I'm glad you two are together, no one can touch you'se now. As the saying goes, united you stand, divided we fall." We both nodded in agreement. We stayed for a while talking to Lee and Terry before Lee suggested we leave. He had to be up early the next day for court and he wanted me to go with him.

The next day I helped Lee up the court steps as his foot was beginning to ache making it hard for him to walk. Once inside we headed to the far end of the courts and sat outside waiting to be called in. Lee liked to 'self medicate' and the damage from the bullet was causing him some serious pain so he started knocking up a joint. I could see the police at the far end of the courts and they were starting to walk towards us as Lee lit his 'bifter.' I made him aware of the police walking towards us. Lee took a long draw and then exhaled. "Fuck them," he said. That was Lee all over.

Lee's case hadn't started on time and the courts were starting to fill up with other cases including a large group of doormen, I'd say there was roughly fifteen of them, and all of them on the gear and big lads. "Those lads down there have been saying they are gonna stop me getting into their club Big Fella. Watch this," said Lee. As quick as a flash he was on his feet and shouting, "Oi Oi." The doormen all looked round. They only knew one man who shouted like that. They looked like school kids in a yard getting told off by their teacher as Lee walked towards them demanding to know which one of them was going to

tell him that he wasn't getting into their club. "You come here," he said to the biggest doorman in the group. The lad had a shaved head and must have been weighing in at about 18 stone. The lad walked towards Lee and he lifted his hand quickly….the doorman almost shit himself as Lee ran his hand through his own hair. He was completely in control here. " Is it you then? Are you going to stop me?" He asked the doorman.
"No mate it wasn't me. I don't want trouble with you." Lee smiled. He had made his point and he would be sure to pay the lads at the club a visit the next time he was in town. A few moments later his name was called out over the tannoy. We were in and out in five minutes as it was just a plea hearing. We had to go back a few weeks later and this time the public gallery was full of the young kids from the snooker hall who were shouting and cheering for their hero! The Magistrate shouted "Stop that shouting and noise or I'll clear the gallery!" On that occasion Lee got bail and all the kids waited outside the court for him. Lee thought it was brilliant. He thanked them all for coming and shook all their hands. The kids respected him because Lee had loads of time for the younger generation.

Despite Lee's injury and trips to court it was still business as usual for us. I got to understand the way Lee's mind worked and got used to his little ways. He loved telling stories and exaggerating. For example if we 'taxed' someone for £2k then he'd put it about that we had taken £20k, or he would tell someone we had knocked out six lads on a job when infact all we had done was give them a verbal warning. He loved hearing these stories being told. It did no harm to be honest and made me laugh. He also loved pretending he was after people to see what their reaction would be. He would say to well known burglar, "Hey you have just burgled my Mam's house." And you would see the lad's face drop. He would try to get me to pretend I was going to thump somebody but I was no good at that kind of thing and my laugh would always give the game away. Lee just loved a good wind up.

I remember one day he picked me up in a really nice convertable car and told me that he had just paid five grand for it . We were driving down Parliament Road in 'Boro when he said, "Fuck it's a nice day Brian, let's get the roof down." Instead of stopping the car, Lee undid the hood whilst we were driving and the hood flew off. I said, "Fucking hell Lee, stop so we can get the hood!" He turned to me and laughed. "Fuck it it's not my car anyway!" It turned out that he had 'taxed' it off someone on his way to see me which was a common occurrence.

On another occasion he had taken a car off someone else. Unfortunately we broke down near the 'Boro stadium. The car had run out of petrol. This was the day that Lee asked me to show the lad we were with how strong I was, so I deadlifted the car before we flagged down a taxi and headed back into 'Boro. The lad had tried to lift the car to but couldn't budge it which Lee found funny. As the taxi pulled into Southbank Lee told the driver to stop. "You're not getting paid mate," said Lee. The driver nodded. This was par for the course with Lee and it was common knowledge between the drivers that if Duffy got in your cab it was for free. After a bite to eat we 'taxed' another car that day and went looking for dealers. The reason we 'borrowed' so many cars was to keep one step ahead of the dealers we were looking for. If we used the same car time and time again then they would know when we were coming.

Another bright idea from Lee, and it has to be said he had a few, he decided to start sending the lad who was driving us around to the dealers door. It was a smart move because they would just think the lad was coming to score drugs. Once the dealer opened the door then bang, we would appear and be on them. We would always make sure there were no women, or kids at these houses. The last thing we wanted was to terrorise families, it was just the lowlife dealers we were interested in. The other reason we used the driver to go to doors for us was because he could run for fun. I wasn't built for chasing dealers around the streets of 'Boro and Lee still had a big hole in his foot and on a few occasions that we had turned up people had run out of their house with the money and gear and got away.

Like any job, the more you do it, the better you get at it and Lee Duffy and I were very strategically minded. Some of the dealers were too and started to get their heads together and notify each other. Whatever area we were in one would alert one another, and say Cockerill and Duffy are about. Everyone would then shut shop wherever we were and go into hiding until we had left and moved onto the next area.

One lad in Redcar got his gate leading up to the door wired up to the electric mains to stop the likes of us coming to his door. The same lad also had a jiff lemon bottle full of amonia. So because of that it became a challenge to Lee. Lee went to 'tax' him one day and waited till the lad was outside the house. The house was in a street that was a dead end at the bottom. Lee jumped out of the car and grabbed the lad by the jumper. The lad in question somehow managed to wriggle his arms out of the jumper and scarper over the wall of the cemetry and over the road. Looking back it was comical as Lee was left holding the lad's jumper and obviously the lad managed to get away.

Most people would have the drugs and money together in those days. So we would get the best of both worlds. Me and Lee only had to slap a few people over this period in time as Lee and I had a fearful reputation that went before us so they would willingly hand over the goods and that way no one got hurt. We never had to carry knives, guns or any other weapons either. To be honest people didn't even put up a fight and no one ever phoned the police to get us arrested. Only once did we ever hear sirens when we on a 'taxing' job and that was at a place in Eston where we had a tip off about a flat above a doctors and a chemist. We went to a door leading to the flat that was really secure. I guess it had to be with it being a doctors and chemist's building. I managed to kick the door through with my size 12's but my leg got trapped as the wood sprung back on my leg. That was when I heard the sirens in the distance. Duffy said "On top! On top" and then Lee and his mate ran off. I was pulling my leg but it was stuck and the harder I pulled the tighter it seemed to get. I could hear Lee and his mate laughing as they ran off! It turned out that the lad upstairs had smashed the chemist window knowing the alarm would go off. I had to smash the door with my hands to release my leg and then I ran back to the car. Lee and his mate had waited for me. "I knew you would get out Big Fella," he said as we drove off. That was a close shave!

    Things went quiet over the next few weeks. It was nice not to have any drama if the truth be told. A few weeks later I was visiting Emma Nixon, who was my girlfriend at the time. She lived in a little bedsit on Newcomen Terrace in Redcar when a car pulled up with two known drug dealers inside. They were from Southbank. Emma seemed to go a little bit on edge. I asked her what was the matter. She explained that they had been coming each day for the lad who had moved in upstairs and they had been banging on Emma's window because she lived in the ground floor flat. The lad upstairs, she said, was a nice lad from Eston called Mally and they had been hounding him for some money he owned and she was terrified. I saw red when I heard this. I watched the lads coming down the path and getting ready to bang on the window. They were surprised to see me appear in the doorway. "Who the fuck do you think you's are coming here?" I said. The stockier one of the two lads tried to front me. He obviously thought he was a bit of a hard case. He went to answer me back but before the first word left his lips I hit him with a left then a right and he was on the floor and out cold. I stood over him and was just about to jump on him and carry on punching him when Emma made me see sense and told me to leave him. I snapped out of the rage and instead noticed a big gold chain round his neck I took it off his neck and said "Don't ever come near here again." His sidekick managed to bring his mate back round before taking him rather gingerly back to the car which I had considered taking from them. Once again though, Emma proved to be the voice of reason. As they drove off Emma shouted upstairs and told Mally that the coast was clear. He came downstairs and Emma introduced him to me. He couldn't thank me enough. I told him that there was no need to thank me and that I was just there to protect Emma, but that if he wanted to repay me that he should make sure Emma was okay when I wasn't around. He told me that he would.

    Over the next few months I got to know Jason 'Mally' Mallet well. I liked him and eventually he started working for me. One night when we were talking he asked me if I could remember the lad that we'd gone to 'tax' in Eston with Lee Duffy at the doctors surgery. I remembered the night of course, how could I forget it? But I hadn't seen the lad's face who we were supposed to be 'taxing,' as he had smashed the window which of course had raised the alarm. "It was me! And it was me who smashed the window," said Mally. You could have knocked me down with a feather. We both laughed out loud as I told him about my leg being stuck in the door.

As time went by Lee and I started going further afield to places like Hartlepool and Billingham. We were kicking doors in all over the place and making a lot of money. This particular day we were in Stockton 'taxing.' We had a tip off that someone had loads of cash in the house in a place called Hardwick. They were big time dealers apparently, the biggest in Stockton at the time. We arrived outside the address. We had someone with us who knew what they looked like and he pointed the main ones out straight away. One of the lads had dark hair and the other blonde. They had been standing in the garden as we had arrived with another four people and when we pulled up they all bolted inside and locked the doors. I headed round the back of the house but the back door was locked too. Lee was still at the front looking through the letterbox and shouting when I noticed that the window was ajar. The two main ones had managed to get out and away and the others were trying to follow. We grabbed a hold of these other lads but they were just visiting the property and had nothing on them. We had been unlucky on this occasion. Our luck hadn't run out though, far from it. Later on that day a few miles from Hardwick we nabbed another couple of dealers and got a thousand ecstasy tablets, a few hundred quid and a couple of mobile phones off them.
Why the mobile phones I hear you ask? To stop them ringing the other dealers on the manor! I told you we were more than pretty faces! We also started 'taxing' the dealers shoes and socks to stop them running off and alerting others. We were learning on every job and making sure we kept one step ahead.

Our next stop off was on Hartington Road in Stockton, where we went to a big old Victorian house. The windows were big old bay windows. We knocked at the door and a lad answered so we walked inside and the lad followed us in. "I'm Lee Duffy and this is Brian Cockerill. Who do you think is the best fighter?" said Lee. The lad looked at Lee and then looked at me. With fear in his eyes he replied "Both of you!" Lee looked at him and smiled. "No, no you can't say that you've got to choose one." The lad looked deflated now realising that no matter what he said it was going to be the wrong answer. Lee then said, "Okay then let me put it this way. Who are you most frightened of then? Me or Brian?" The lad kept looking from me to Lee and then said, "Fuck this." With that he took a run straight for the window and jumped right through it. It was like a scene out of a film. There was glass everywhere. With the kid gone Lee picked the television up. "What you gonna do with that?" I said. " Sell it!" was Lee's reply as we walked out the front door and back to the car. Our driver that day couldn't believe what he had just witnessed. He thought we had thrown him out until we told him what exactly had happened.

The next 'tax' was only a few streets away where we scored a nine bar and five hundred quid. The kid had a bit of personal left in his pockets but I let him keep that and he thanked me which really tickled Lee. We had just gone into his home, taxed his drugs and cash and he thanked us. "You couldn't script that" said Lee.

It wasn't always that easy though. I was told a story by John Mcpartland who was Kev Kilty's brother-in-law. He was from Whinney Banks and was a well known armed robber and a convicted drug dealer. His nickname was Mac and he didn't give a fuck . One day Duffy went to his house but Mac had been tipped off by Kev Kilty that Duffy was coming to 'tax' him. When Duffy arrived Mac invited him in. "I wanna word with you," said Duffy as he walked into his home. " Cup of tea?" Replied Mac. Lee looked a bit puzzled at his response and said, " I don't think you understand Mac, I've come to 'tax' you and take your money." Mac remained unflustered and said to Lee, "Okay give me a minute will you." He went into the kitchen and came back out with a 4:10 shotgun. "Tax me? I'll blow ya fucking head off!" Duffy jumped up and ran out of the house. Mac followed him out with the gun and Lee jumped in his car and sped off.

It was probably experiences like this and the fact that he had been shot on more than one occasion that made Lee frightened of guns and was why he would often send me to go and boot doors in first when we went 'taxing' together but I never thought anything of it to be honest. I was just thinking of the money and not about who might be waiting to stop us. Call it bravery or stupidity but I just didn't give a fuck.

Chapter Seven: Jail Tales

Lee told me lots of stories from the lengthy time he spent in many of the jails across the country so I thought I would share a few with you.
In one of his earliest sentences in Durham jail when Lee was in his early twenties at the time, he spent time with a notorious prisoner by the name of Paul Sykes. Paul was a renowned fighting man and had won the Koestler award for his book 'Sweet Agony.' Rumours had been circulating for a while that he had been sleeping with young men in prison and there were allegations of rape which were later verified by prison officers. I wasn't a fan of Sykes either. In 1993 I went to fight him in Wakefield and he wouldn't come out of the pub! His reputation was built on rumours that he started. Even in the ring he was a coward. In one fight he turned his back on Geordie fighter John L Gardner. He used to get stick for that in jail as prisoners would say "Watch your back Sykesy, John L Gardner's behind you." He never lived that down.

Like any right minded soul Lee hated 'nonces' and as you will know sex offenders are hated amongst cons and are kept on separate wings in jail. One day Lee was being moved from one wing to another. The screws had always kept Duffy and Sykes apart but on this day Sykes had requested a move too and they crossed paths on the landing. Lee saw the beast and shouted "Fucking rapist, fucking nonce! Come on Sykes, fight me you fucking sex case. You're a paedo, you fucking beast." By now Lee had his hands up as he was screaming and was calling Sykes every name possible to entice him to fight but Sykes hung his head in shame as the prison officers surrounded Duffy and stood between the pair. The officers transferring Sykes managed to get him along the landing and onto the next wing, leaving a frustrated Duffy cursing him. That was his only chance to serve out some prison justice to a man some retarded people hero worship still to this day. Sykes was shipped out of the prison soon after for breaking the jaws of three officers. According to witnesses the screws had come for Sykes ten minutes late for exercise in the gym. He used to train on the weights and the boxing bag. When the hour exercise was up the screws told everyone to finish off but Sykes insisted on having the ten minutes extra that he was owed for them being late. There was a stand off and then when they rushed him he battered them.

When Lee was in Leeds jail it was approaching lunch time by the time he got through reception and to his pad. The young lad he was to be padded up with said "Now then Lee" as he walked in and put his stuff on his bunk. The lad was from 'Boro but he didn't know him. Lee asked the lad if he had any baccy. The lad told him he didn't but he did have some 'tac' to smoke. So Lee gave him some baccy and papers and asked the lad to knock him a joint up. The lad obliged. As they sat and smoked the joint, two orderlies came to the cell door. They were both rastafarians, both over six feet tall and well built. One of them pipes up "Where's our money?" Duffy's new pad mate replied "I'm on a visit tomorrow I will have it for you then." This didn't go down well at all with the two rastas. Duffy is sitting watching and listening. The other orderly then says "We told you today. You're gonna get it." As quick as they had arrived they had gone. The lad from 'Boro was as white as a ghost and shaking. Lee asked him what it was all about and he told him that he owed them money for the gear they were smoking. They finished the joint just as dinner was called. "Come on" said Lee. The lad shook his head. " I'm not going. Those lads run this jail, they are going to kick the fuck out of me." Lee gave him a look and smiled. " You just come with me. You'll be alright." Still rather reluctantly the lad stood up and then they headed onto the landing and down to the serving plate for dinner where they joined the queue. Sure enough the two rastas started walking over towards them. Under his breath Lee told the lad to move to the side. The two rastas started shouting, "We want our fucking money." As they got next to the young lad from 'Boro one of the rastas went to grab him. It would be the last thing he would remember. Lee left hooked one and knocked him clean out and he hit the other with a right which floored him. Both rastas were completely unconcious. The screws came running over and Lee was taken down the block. His visit to Leeds would be a short one. He was moved out to another jail soon after. It was something Lee was used to, having done time in over twenty jails.

Chris Curry spent time in Holmehouse prison with me in 2010 but had done Borstal with Lee as kid. He would often say that Duffy reminded him of the fictional character 'Carling' from the film 'Scum'. Chris would often recall how Lee would take over in the gym and would have the lads doing circuits. On one occasion in the gym Lee said to three lads, "You three stand there and when I say go I want you to do cartwheels across the hall." He then got another three and said, "Stand there and when I say go you three, do ballerina spins," and he said to another six, "When I say go, you do wheelbarrows," and finally he said to the remaining lads, "The rest of you run across to that wall and back." The kids were too frightened to say no and the screw would sit back and watch as Duffy took his 'class' for thirty minutes. Well they do say healthy body healthy mind!

It has been well documented in the book 'The Sayers Tried And Tested At The Highest Level' and in 'Operation Sayers' that Lee Duffy was very good friends with Stephen and Michael Sayers. Lee met Stephen in borstal and they hit it off immediately. Birds of a feather certainly flock together. On one occasion Stephen recalls Lee walking up to a screw and telling the officer to give him a cigarette. The screw explained that he only had one left. So Lee gave him that look and said, " Well give me that, and when you go on your lunch go and get me another twenty." The screw pulled the packet of cigarettes out of his pocket and handed it to Lee who smiled and turned his back. A couple of hours later, after lunch there was a knock at Lee's cell door. The screw from earlier walked in and handed a fresh pack of twenty tabs to Lee. You see even the screws were petrified of Duffy. It is one of the reasons he spent time in so many prisons. He would arrive, kick off and then be shipped out. He was just too hard to handle.

Chapter Eight: Taxing Our Way To The Top

The drug dealers were stepping up their game. Instead of having the drugs and money together in the same house they started keeping them in different locations. So we had to up our game too. We started targeting the street dealers. We would grab a hold of one and get them to tell us what day and time the supplier was going to drop their stuff off. They would tell us and we would then be there to 'tax' the supplier. We would reward the dealer for the tip off. So let's say we took 9 ounces of blow off a supplier, then we would give the street dealer an ounce for his trouble. This way of working saw our profits rocket. We were all winners, except the suppliers and nobody had the bravery to confront me or Lee. One of Redcar's C.I.D jokingly said to me, "You two are like the Mafia. You've taken over the whole area and nobody can stop you."

Emma told me of one night at 'Ramsey's Blues.' I wasn't with her that night but Lee was there with some lads from Sheffield that he had been with the night before. At one point that night Emma went to the toilets, which were in the back of the house and she saw one of the lads from Yorkshire was carrying a gun in the waist of his jeans. Shortly afterwards Lee said to one of the lads he was with, "I bet you can't knock him out," and pointed to a lad stood across from the group. One of the group decided to give it a go. The poor, innocent bystander was hit with a right hander and hit the floor but was quick to regain his composure and get back on his feet a little dazed. Lee shook his head and laughed. "I will show you how to do it properly!" With that he banged the same lad again this time knocking him out. Emma headed off into the other room after, leaving the boys to be boys.

Later that night there was more trouble at the blues and a gun had been discharged. Emma was still in there she spoke to 'Joof' who used to take the money on the door and Ramsey to see what had happened they told her that Lee had pulled the trigger of his mates gun and it had left a hole in the toilet door. That hole remained there until the place closed a few years later.

Lee and his friends were still on it the following day and were in a pub in Eston. They were all sniffing coke and playing cards around a table. One of the Sheffield lads pulled out the same gun. It was a six shooter. He then proceeded to take the bullets out of the gun and replaced one bullet back in and spun the barrel. He put the gun to his head and pulled the trigger. Lee was laughing and said, "I bet you daren't do that again." The lad wasn't going to back down so he spun the barrel of the gun and did it again. His luck was in, the gun selected an empty chamber. These were the kind of people Lee was mixing with. They just did not give a fuck. The lads headed home the next day and I never saw Lee till the end of that week as he caught up on his sleep and dealt with a come down.

We had a bit of work later that week. Me and Mark met Lee at his mam's house. We picked him up and he looked fresh. As we were driving through Southbank we came to a crossing. Mark stopped to let a couple of lads across. Mark was just about to pull away when Lee said, "Wait." He then jumped out of the car and said to one of the lads, "Oi do you remember me you bastard?" Then he banged the lad and knocked him out on the crossing. Lee got back in the car while the lad's mate was trying to pick him up. I said to Lee, "Fucking hell what was all that about?" Lee explained to me that he had been bullied at school and that over the last few years he had tracked each of his tormentors down and given them a taste of their own medicine. The lad at the crossing had been the ringleader so had given Lee extra satisfaction. It was something that I could relate to having been bullied myself as a child. I told Lee that I had in fact done exactly the same as him and had eventually given the bully a taste of his own medicine.

    Sharing our experiences seemed to bring us closer and helped us form a stronger bond. We both opened up about the fears we had as kids in bed at night worrying about what was going to happen to us at school. Let that be a lesson to any bully out there. The kid you are bullying won't always be that little mild mannered kid. Some day he might turn out to be like me and Lee and woe betide you!

    We headed to Redcar for some fish and chips after that incident with the thought of the job in the back of our minds. Lee got a small fish and chips whilst I got fish and chips, a pattie and a sausage. I always seemed to eat twice as much as Lee and if there was anything left of his then I'd usually eat that too. With our bellys filled and the world put to right we took a trip to the Marske and Saltburn area as we had quite a few tip offs of addresses where people were selling blow.

    The first address we turned up at was a big Victorian building which had been turned into flats. The supposed dealers flat was on the bottom floor. When we got into the flat this lad had coin bags and a ruler and the gear on the table. We got just under 9oz which was about £100 per ounce in those days. He must have been quite new at the game as back then not a lot of dealers kept scales with the gear because if you got caught with them there was more chance of going to jail. If the gear was for personal use you wouldn't need scales. What people did was use a ruler, balance it on something and put coins like a two pence coin on one side and the gear on the other side and when it balanced equally that was the weight. We sold his gear for £700 and followed that up with a couple more small 'taxes' and made another £300. With a few quid in our pocket we decided to have a drive over to Stockton to pick Craig Howard up. Craig was pleased to see us. We all jumped in his car as he had just bought a top of the range BMW and wanted to show it off to us. Craig could drive for fun and if it ever came on top (which it did on several occasions) then Craig would leave the cop cars for dead.

    Next stop that day was Newcastle where we headed to a well known face's house. Lee had a lot of connections in Newcastle and this man was pleased to see him. It turned out that Lee had served a bit of time with him. The man knew Craig too. Lee asked the man if he had any gear and he told us to wait two minutes and headed out into his back garden. I thought that Lee meant blow when he asked for gear but when the man came came back inside he had a big bag of white powder. I didn't know what it was until Lee told me that it was cocaine. The man said to Lee, "Do you lads want a line?" and he proceeded to knock four long thick lines up. He then got a tenner out of his pocket, rolled it up and put it to his nose and snorted it. Then Lee and Craig did the same. They then handed me the rolled up note. I said, "No not for me I don't take drugs." Lee and Craig looked at each other and then started egging me on saying, "Come on we'll have a laugh today."

So with a bit of peer pressure I took my first recreational drug. It went up my nose easy enough and then as I swallowed there was a horrible taste at the back of my throat and it felt numb for a few minutes. Other than that I felt no different at all. We stayed a while at this mans house chatting and then Lee handed the man £700 and in return the man handed him a big bag of coke. We then had another line each before we left. Craig and Lee were in the front of the car and I got in the back. I then remember laughing out loud for no reason. Lee looked round and asked me what was up. I said, "I don't see what all the fuss is about with this coke lads. I don't even think it's working on me?" At that Lee and Craig burst into fits of laughter Lee had tears rolling down his face as he was laughing that much. He said, "Not working? You've never shut up for over two hours! We haven't been able to get a word in edgeways." So it clearly had worked!

On the way back to 'Boro we stopped at a shop and bought some bottles of pop, some pens, and a few other bits and bobs and we went back to Craig's house and straight into the back kitchen. Craig got a test tube out and held it with a clamp and he put some cocaine and some bicarb in and a bit of water and he held it over the gas stove. I was thinking what the fuck is he doing he looked like a mad professor in a lab. He then got a metal coat hanger and put it into the test tube where the stuff started sticking to it. He then blew on it a few times. It was now rock hard. We all went to the table where Craig scraped the stuff onto a yellow pages book. Lee was putting something together with a bottle, pen and foil. He then got the ash off some cigarettes and put it on the foil and put a small amount of the stuff from the yellow pages book on top. Lee went first, then Craig then me. I hadn't a clue what I was supposed to do. Lee was telling me to suck through the pen and hold it in, so I gave it a big suck. After that I didn't know where I was for a few moments. We all walked into the living room and slumped down into the chairs.

It was this day that Lee opened up and talked to me for the first time about our first encounter. He said, "You know that day Bri you had me beat. If it wasn't for John Fail that day I was fucked. I have never fought anyone with your strength. It was terrifying and everyone I've hit with that type of punch I hit

didn't get back up. You were like a mad bull."
I started to feel a little bit paranoid as Lee was talking. It felt like it was leading to something. It didn't help being on crack for the first time. I nodded and listened to what he was saying and then told him to forget about it and that it was in the past and that we were a good team and good friends now. He looked at me and then put his arms around me and said, "I love ya mate. On my daughters life I will never do anything like that again." I could see in his eyes that he was being genuine. He continued, " Every time you kick a door in your putting yourself on the line for me and I will for you. You don't give a fuck Big Fella." He then turned to Craig and started telling him how fast my hands were for my size he said, "Craig you can't be that size and that fast it beats the laws of physics.!" He then asked me to give Craig a demonstration. Lee got Craig's gloves and pads out. I put the gloves on and started throwing lefts and rights and Duffy was shouting that the power was unreal. I was still feeling paranoid so I passed the gloves to Craig. Lee still had the pads on and Craig began punching them. His punches were straight and stiff. "You're best sticking to bodybuilding Craig," said Lee and we all started laughing. Lee was always making people laugh.

   Then Lee asked me to hold the pads for him. He put the gloves on and I was thinking here we go, is this a set up? He threw some shots at the pads and the power and accuracy was unreal as was the speed. After about ten shots I said, "Come on let's have a bit more of that stuff." I was hooked. We stayed at Craig's till about two in the morning and then decided to go to one of Lee's mates houses. This lad used to drive Lee around and lived in Grangetown. We all had another go of the pipe at this lads house and Lee then went to the toilet. When he came back there had been a change in his mood and he looked angry. He said, "Right who's took half of that gear off the table?" There was an awkward silence and then he said, "Before we go any further I know it's not you Big Fella." He then said the same to the other lad there and then turned to Craig. "So Craig that leaves you." Lee wasn't shouting and bawling he was just talking but you could of cut the atmosphere with a knife. Whenever Lee was having a go at anyone he always remained calm. A bit like a pro boxer does before a fight, He had obviously mastered the art of it. If you lose your temper you produce adrenalin when this happens then you run out of breath quicker.

   I decided to try and mediate between Lee and Craig and said, "Leave it Lee, he won't have pinched it." Lee was still looking at Craig and replied, "Believe me Big Fella if I'm wrong I will apologise. Get your clothes off Craig." Craig held his hands up and said, "I wouldn't do that mate." I have to be honest I believed what Craig was saying and I told Lee that I thought asking Craig to strip off was going too far. Craig wasn't concerned in the slightest and proceeded to take his clothes off and was stood in his underwear a few seconds later. Lee looked straight at him. "Get them off." he said pointing to his underpants. As he pulled them to the side a big rock fell out onto the floor. I couldn't believe it. Lee moved forward to give Craig a slap but thought better of it and stopped himself. "Go on just fuck off" he said. It was quite clear that the betrayal had hurt him. Still quite calm he turned and said to me, "See what did I tell you Big Fella, he's tried to nick £100 worth of gear." as Craig bundled his clothes up and ran out of the door and back to his car. We spent another couple of hours there and finished the gear. With Craig gone I had no transport home so we crashed at Lee's mates house. I slept on the floor and Lee slept on the sofa. When I woke up the next day I felt like shit so we went to a local cafe for breakfast so I could try and pull myself around. From there we went to see Lee's girlfriend who was about to have a baby any day. We stayed there for about an hour. Lee got a photo of her before he left as he was getting a picture of her tattooed on his arm that day.

      We went to 'Scorpios' for the tattoo and there was a few waiting. "I'm next," Lee said as we walked in. There were no complaints. We were in there a few hours whilst Lee got her face on his arm. The lad made a good job of it and told Lee it was 'on the house.' As we headed out of the tattoo parlour which was near Middlesbrough bus station we saw our mates Tommy Harrison and Buster walking towards us. As I have already said Lee loved a laugh. He said, "You get one side Bri and I'll get the other and pretend we are fighting." I was up for this so I went over to the opposite side to Lee and I shouted, "Come on Duffy." Lee then started shouting, "Come on Cockerill let's get this sorted once and for all." Whilst we were doing this Lee's driver the young lad who was in on the joke was pretending to keep us apart. Tommy Harrison started coming towards us and had panic in his face. "Come on lads leave it, I thought you two were mates? Behave lads you're in the town centre. You's will get locked up." We had turned it up a notch and were both jumping around and then we both burst out laughing. Tommy called us all bastards as me and Lee hugged each other still giggling. After a catch up with Tommy and Buster Lee dropped me back home. It was good to be back in my own bed. My first experience on drugs had certainly been eventful.

Chapter Nine: Good Cop, Bad Cop

I went to see a friend one day with Kevin Kilty called Datchi Thompson. He had been out the previous night for a meal in a pub with a girl and John and Maureen Mcpartland and were at a pub in Middlesbrough. Their car was parked in the pub carpark and as he and his girlfriend were leaving she said there's Lee Duffy. Duffy had tried to 'tax' Datchi on more than one occasion and he had been making his mouth go about Duffy to anyone who would listen to him. Duffy was walking straight towards his car so Datchi decided to drive straight at Lee. The car wasn't going that fast so Lee dived on the bonnet of the car and hung onto the windscreen wipers. Lee shouted, "Stop the fucking car." Datchi had not expected that reaction from Lee and was panicking now and came to an abrupt stop. Lee jumped off the car and opened the driver's door and dragged Datchi out and gave him a right hander. He then emptied Datchis pockets. Datchi always had a few quid on him as he was a known drug dealer in Thornaby. Lee then turned his back and walked off and was shouting "I'm coming to your house next." Datchi was just counting his blessings that Lee had just hit him the once as he got back in his car and drove home. When Kevin and I arrived at Datchi's house he came out of his front door in a a total state of panic with a big black eye from his run in with Lee. He was speaking at a hundred miles an hour and started rambling about shooting Lee if he turned up. He said, "If I get life I get life." Me and Kevin managed to calm him down and I told him that I would go and see Lee and try to sort it out for him.

I got Kevin to drop me back home and I jumped in my car which was a yellow Vauxhall SRI that I had just bought. I then drove to see Lee in Eston where he was at his girlfriend's house. Lee came out and got in the car. I explained that I had just been to see Datchi and I asked him if he would do me a favour and leave him alone. I explained that Datchi wasn't a bad lad. Lee listened to what I had to say and then said, "He's a cheeky little cunt Bri, shouting he's gonna do this and do that when he sees me." He was right of course but I tried again and explained that he was sorry for what he had said and that he had been 'off his head' on drugs and wasn't being himself when he was saying those things. I also explained that he was worried sick that Lee was going to go to his house because he had two young kids. Lee smiled and said, "Ok I will leave him alone but he's not getting the £600 back I taxed off him last night. And you can tell him that I'm only leaving him alone for you Big Fella" We shook hands and Lee, who started laughing said, "Now you're coming with me for a Parmo on Datchi!"

We headed to one of Lee's mates houses to pick him up and then pulled in at a garage to fill the car up. Lee paid for the petrol and got some cigarette papers and started knocking a joint up in the car. I said, "You're not smoking that stuff again are ya ?" He told me he was and that it was Datchi's fault because when he had 'taxed' him and taken his money he had also taken some blow off him too. We all started laughing again as I pulled off the garage forecourt. Come to think of it, I laughed a lot with Lee. Never a day went by when we didnt laugh and joke. I suggested we drove to Datchi's to put his mind at rest. Lee agreed and we set off for Thornaby where he lived. We pulled up outside the house and I got out of the car. Lee stayed in the car as I knocked on the door. Datchi opened the door and I had just started explaining the situation when next thing his Mrs flew out of the door screaming and shouting at Duffy and telling him to get away from her house. She was hysterical and was waving her arms around saying, "Dont think he's coming in here." I told Datchi to shut her up because I was doing him a favour bringing Lee to shake his hand and get everything sorted. He could see I was genuine and he shouted at his Mrs to get inside and to leave it. Once she was back inside I waved at Lee and told him to come over. Lee got out of the car and we all went into the house. Lee was calm again despite the provovation from Datchi's Mrs. They shook hands and Lee apologised for batting Datchi in the mouth but told him in no uncertain terms that he shouldn't have been running his mouth off. Datchi agreed with Lee and admitted that he deserved a bat in the mouth for what he had been saying. We stayed for a while and shared a few tales and had a laugh and then got on our way.

    I went back to Datchi's the next day with Kevin Kilty and Datchi thanked me for mediating and his Mrs apologised for her behaviour. I told her to forget about it and was pleased everything had worked out in the end. Datchi was involved in a car crash a few months later with his friends Tommo and Elvis and he ended up paralysed from the neck down. Sadly he died as a result of his injuries.

    After the incident with Datchi we had a tip off about a house in Netherfields where a lad was apparently selling a lot of blow from a downstairs flat. We pulled up outside and walked up the path and knocked on the door. A lad answered and we went inside. There was a big fish tank in the living room full of fish. We told him that we had come to 'tax' him. He was quite calm and without hesitation he handed us about two and a half ounces of blow and a couple of deals that had already been made up. Lee wasn't satisfied with that and asked him where his money was as we had been told what he had just been dropped off. The kid's face changed realising that someone close to him had been making his mouth go about his business. Lee and I then went into a good cop, bad cop routine. Something we used to do on a regular basis. Lee said, "Look just tell me where it is as you don't want him kicking off and giving you a slap." I then started shouting at him saying telling him that I would smash his fucking face in. It was all part of the blag. Lee then carried on telling me to calm down and telling me that the lad would sort it and that I should stand in the passage way. I flew back in and told the lad that if he didn't do what we wanted that I would stick his head in the fish tank. That did the trick as he explained that the money wasn't in the house but was at his sister's on Parliament Road. With that revelation we got him in the car and took a drive to his sisters house. When we arrived on the street he pointed a house out and we pulled over. He got out of the car and went into the house and quickly came back out with £650. He handed it to me through the window, looked at me and Lee and said "How will I get home?" Lee threw him twenty quid and said, "Here, get a taxi" and we drove off. We split the money 50-50 and I told Lee to keep the blow we had got off the lad so he insisted I take more of the money but I told him that it was okay.

Chapter Ten: Meeting The Sayers

One day we were driving through Linthorpe village in Middlesbrough when Lee asked me to pull over. "I'm just gonna run in the gym and see someone," he said. I offered to go in with him but he told me that he was okay and would only be a couple of minutes so I stayed in the car. When Lee came back to the car he seemed a little bit out of breath so I asked him what had happened. Lee said, "I've just had to knock two lads out who tried to stop me getting in the gym. Nobody stops me getting in nowhere." I offered to go back in with him but he told me to drive off as they would probably have phoned the police.

'The Mall' in Stockton had won awards four years in a row for being a top nightclub and the doorman who worked there were probably the biggest doorman around at the time. They were all bodybuilders and boxers who could have a fight. They had been quoted on many occasions saying that if Lee Duffy tried to go to the club, he would get a kicking. Lee got wind of this and as you know Lee loved a challenge so Lee and Craig turned up at the Mall in shorts, t-shirt and trainers. The dress code was strictly smart, ie trousers, shoes and a shirt. The biggest doorman at the club was a lad called Rob. He was a six foot four bodybuilder and was at the entrance with another three doorman when Lee and Craig walked straight to the entrance and just walked past them. Once inside the door there was a kiosk where people paid to get in where another four doorman would be stood. Realising who had just walked in Rob the bodybuilder and the doorman from outside came in and Rob said, "You can't come in dressed like that." Lee smiled as he always did and replied to Rob, "Are you gonna stop me like? What's your name? I'm Lee Duffy." Rob's bottle had gone and he was speechless along with the other doorman who were looking to him for leadership. Lee seeing that Rob had lost it said, "Your working under false pretences. I've asked you your name and you don't even know it."
Lee and Craig then turned their backs on the door team and walked past the kiosk and straight into the club and got a drink. After about half an hour the manager and owner went up to Lee and said look can we have a meeting tomorrow at the Swallow Hotel as obviously none of my door staff have the capabilities to stop you coming in. Lee agreed and carried on drinking with Craig.

The next day Lee and Craig went to the Swallow Hotel to meet the owner as arranged. The manager told him that he was willing to pay him a 'considerable' amount of money to stay away from the venue and he had brought the cash with him. Lee shook the managers hand and took the money and told him that he would never see him again. Lee kept his word. The only club where the doorstaff actually stood up to Lee was the Bongo in Middlesbrough. The doormen there couldn't fight Lee in a fight, but all the doormen in there, and Abduli the owner were always tooled up with hammers, machetes, bats and the like. Abduli had even chased Lee with a machete once. Elvis and Tomo got jumped by the doorman there too, who used a hammer to smash Tomo over the head. I was in the car with Elvis a short time after the incident and he spotted one of the doorman who had hit him with a hammer. He jumped out of the car and both of them had a fist fight. Tomo was boxing at the time and he caught the doorman with a left hook and left him sparked out in the street. Elvis said, "You're not so clever now without your hammer".

One Saturday Lee turned up at the Bongo alone and tried to get in and the doormen attacked him with knives and other weapons. Lee didn't hang around. Instead he rounded up two cars full of lads the following night all with balaclavas, all tooled up and all with bad intentions. Lee made sure he had an alibi and had headed to Newcastle whilst his pals all waited for the doormen to finish. If it all came on top then Lee would have been prime suspect. He wasn't stupid. The lads beat the fuck out of the doorman and smashed them to pieces. There was one casualty with one of Lee's mates sustaining a bad cut on his leg but it didn't take away the sweet taste of victory.

Bryan Flartey was a good friend to me and Lee and on many occasions after a night out we would end up at his house. He was a top man and very friendly. It was Flartey who mentioned his connections in Newcastle with the Sayers family. He told us that they 'ran' Newcastle and were the biggest crime family in the City. Lee started telling us about Stephen, Michael and John and said that he had met them in jail. He said, "They are just like us Big Fella. They hate grasses and if you're their friend then your their friend for life." Lee had mentioned me to them and they were apparently dying to meet me. He had told them about our fight and that I was the hardest and strongest man he had ever fought. I told Lee that I would happily go over to Newcastle with him to meet them.

After we left Bryan's we went to the blues and Lee was encouraging me to do my party piece which was picking up cars by the rear end like a deadlift. Lee was fascinated at my strength. This night he was telling everyone to come outside and watch me do it. By now we had a big crowd outside and Lee said, "Show them how strong you are Big Fella." So I bent down and put my hands under the bumper and lifted this car several times. Lee was beaming and saying, "I told ya! I told ya how strong he was." Most places we went for a drink he would have me doing it but I didn't mind.

A week later we went to Stokesly for a night out where a lot of travellers stay, to see Dickie Dido who used to take us on the pads at the gym. We were having a great night and we went to every pub on the High Street and we had all had a good drink. Lee introduced me to a really good friend of his, Mark Hartley. Mark's a lovely lad. We were all laughing and joking, but you always get one person who tries to spoil a good night and this one gobshite was trying to wind me and Lee up and trying to goad us to fight. Lee just blanked him but I started getting angry and this lad was really getting to me. I told the lad to shut up and that he was wasting his time trying to stir things up between me and Lee as we were pals but the lad wouldn't listen. I warned him again to shut his mouth but he was still going on. Next thing I know Dido has jumped up and hit the lad with a hell of a body shot and threw him out of the pub. We never saw the lad again. We went on to have a great night and sure enough Lee had me doing my party piece again on Stokesly High Street.

When I eventually met Stephen and Michael Sayers we hit it off really well. Lee was right, they were my kind of people and it is a friendship that has stood the test of time. On my first trip to the 'Toon' Stephen had picked me up and was keen to introduce me to various friends and family members. After that we went for a meal but when we came back out to the car we realised it had a puncture. As Stephen was trying to work out what he could do I asked him if he had a jack. He looked in the boot. He didn't have one but he did have a wheel brace. I told him to take the nuts off the wheel and replace it with his spare as soon as I lifted his car. Stephen looked at me like I had two heads, not quite believing what I had just said. There was an old cloth in the boot which I wrapped my hands with and I lifted the car off the ground for Stephen to change the wheel. He couldn't believe what he was seeing and kept asking me if I was alright. I told him I was fine and that if he'd just get it changed I would be a lot better! He started laughing. From that day on whenever I was out with Stephen, yes you've guessed it, he had me doing the same party piece that Lee had me doing.

Stephen did go one step further than Lee one night when he asked me how strong I really was. There were seven cars in the street so I went behind each of the cars and moved them all one by one so that they all ended up pointing sideways. We were both laughing out loud thinking about people going back to their cars and seeing them all pointing in a different direction to how they had left them.

Another well known name in Newcastle at that time was Viv Graham. He ran the doors up there and was a tough fighting man. I had been offered the chance to fight 'Viv,' so travelled to Tyneside and met up with the Sayers and headed to one of the clubs he had, 'Madisons.' We got there as arranged but there was no sign of him. He had obviously 'cocked' and not fancied it. We tried to arrange another fight at a venue on the Quayside and we were going to sell tickets to watch. Stephen Sayers agreed to put up £50k prize money but not even that brought 'Viv' to the table. I asked Stephen years later who he thought would have won the fight and he said, "I wouldn't have put the money up If I didn't think you were going to win mate." Stephen also had my back along with Andrew Atkinson from Roseworth and Basil from 'Boro when I went to fight Dave Garside. You just cannot buy loyalty like that.

I think a lot of the laughter and fun that Lee Duffy had with the Sayers gave him a different outlook on life. He seemed to enjoy his nights in Newcastle more than 'Boro. Looking back I don't think any of us had really grown up. We were all full of mischief and up for a laugh. Me and Emma are still the same today in a lot of ways. Stephen Sayers is too. He came to my house in 2019 with our good friend Steve Wraith when he saw an ornament on our sitting room table of a baby silverback gorilla. Stephen said to Emma, "Aw is that Brian as a baby?" Funny, very funny.

Chapter Eleven: The Greatest Fight That Never Happened

Lee Duffy told me about the day he went to Newcastle to have a fight with Viv Graham. It was a Sunday night and he had met up with Stephen Sayers. They were going around town looking for 'Viv' and going to all of the doors that he ran and asking if he was there. They arrived at 'Macey's' on the Groat Market and the five lads there started to square up to him. He knocked four of them out and they were rolling around on the floor like baby dinosaurs. He turned to the fifth doorman and said, "I'm gonna leave you awake cause my names the 'Duffer' and I want to fight your boss. Tell 'Viv' Graham that Lee Duffy's here now and I want to fight him." Word got round Newcastle that night but Lee never caught up with 'Viv' that night.

Stephen spoke to both parties and was trying to arrange a winner takes all fight between the pair with £20k for the winner. Lee was well up for it but 'Viv' was avoiding him like the plague. Instead 'Viv's doormen were copping for a sore jaw on his doors as Lee kept knocking them out each time he visited Newcastle. So Viv Graham went to see John Brian Sayers.

John is Stephen, Michael and John's Dad. After John Snr invited him in, 'Viv' explained that he was doing well with his doors now, employing over one hundred men and he did not want the hassle with Lee and did not want to fight him. John tried to persuade him to think again advising him that a straightener would be the best way to sort it out and that he could guarantee any fight would be fair and would be one on one, but 'Viv' wasn't interested and asked John to call Lee and tell him that he did not want to fight him.

So John phoned Lee up, explained the situation and told him that 'Viv' was alongside him and had told him that if he wants to say he is the best fighter then so be it. Lee was not happy and said, "Tell him from me that he has to fight me. He's got no choice. He has to fight me he's bullied people for years and he knows what I'm on about. I want to fight him. I'll fight him anywhere he wants. Put him on the phone please John." John handed the phone to 'Viv,' "He wants to speak to you son." 'Viv' just looked away. John put the phone back to his ear and said "He doesn't want to speak to you Lee." It would go down in history as the greatest fight that never happened.

'Viv' was later jailed for the incident at 'Hobos' in Newcastle with Stephen Sayers, which you can read about in Stephen's book, 'The Sayers Tried And Tested At The Highest Level.'. At that time John Mcpartland and Herby Clarke were running the other wing in Durham and decided to wind 'Viv' up by pretending to stage a riot. So they started banging and making noise and throwing a few things so 'Viv' goes storming over and tells them that if they don't pack it in then they will have him to answer to. They started laughing as he walked off knowing that their plan to wind him up had worked like a treat. The screws had seen what had gone on and praised him and he apparently got a reduction on his sentence for stopping a riot! Unbelievable.

I actually saw Viv in the jail and he waved at me. Then he sent a message asking me to go to the gym to train with him but I never took him up on the offer. He wasn't well liked in the prison system. People found him quite arrogant and a bit of a bully. One Scottish prisoner said to me that 'Viv' thought he ran the jail but he didn't. I was only in that jail a week before I moved on.

Chapter Twelve: The 'Real' Lee Duffy

Me and Lee had been out taxing all day up in the sticks at the likes of Loftus, Brotton and Saltburn. We had made a few quid and we went home to get changed and arranged to meet back up on the night and have a night out in Middlesbrough. Lee turned up to meet me in a small white car and we went to see our friend Bry Flartey again. We had a few drinks at Flarteys house then Lee said that he wanted to go to the 'Havana'.

Once in the club Lee handed me a tablet and said, "Here take this Big Fella." It was called a 'mitsy' short for Mitsubishi, which was a type of ecstasy tablet. They had become really popular amongst clubbers and I was about to take my first one. At first I felt okay and nothing had changed at all. Then I started to feel a bit strange and I looked around for Lee who was cossack dancing on the dancefloor. He then started doing one legged squats and then a spot of shadow boxing. I was feeling red hot and felt dizzy. I was all over the place so I decided to sit on a bar stool. I literally couldn't move. Lee must have seen that I wasn't quite right so he put my arm over his shoulder and helped me out of the club. He put me in the car and asked me if I was okay or did I feel a bit hot and paranoid? I told him I did but he reassured me and said that he would look after me. Lee drove us to another club on Linthorpe Road but I couldn't move as my legs were like jelly and to be truthful I was still feeling paranoid. Lee went inside for a bit and then came back to the car to check on me and then went back inside. When he came back out again I was feeling a bit better but to be honest the rest of that night is a complete blur. I can't remember where we ended up but Lee said I had a good time!

It took me a few days in bed to get over that first ecstasy because the comedown was horrible. I didn't want to face the world. I was paranoid, restless, and my temperature was up and down. It wasn't a pleasant experience. So anyone thinking of taking drugs? My advice is don't bother! I wouldn't advise anyone to take them. They completely fry your brain one minute and you're high as a kite and the next minute you feel suicidal.

As I had been recovering I didn't see Lee for a few days. It was about five days later when Craig Howard called round and told me that Lee's girlfriend had given birth to a little girl. We headed to 'Moore's' gym first for a workout and then after training we popped over to Lee's to see him and his new family. Lee was overjoyed and very proud. There is a photo you will all have seen of him holding the baby and that was taken the same day. Lee was really emotional but so happy and he kept saying "Look at the size of her!" You could see the love for the baby in his eyes and he couldn't stop looking at her. I gave him a big cuddle and congratulated him.

We decided to have a run over to 'Boro and see a well known black lad who was a good friend of Lee's called Jimmy Murray. He made us a nice curry, and Lee and Jimmy had a couple of joints. I moaned about him smoking and he laughed, which was par for the course. From there we went to see another mutual friend of ours called Shaun in Lingdale. When we got there John Fail was with him. The lads said we needed to 'wet the babies head' so we had a quick catch up and arranged to meet in 'Boro later for a drink. We had a great night out and no trouble. I have read a lot of reports and stories saying Lee did this and Lee did that in 'Boro but most of it is rubbish. Whenever Lee and I were together in pubs and clubs in Middlesbrough we always had fun and Lee was always polite to people and he certainly didn't hit anyone for no reason when I was with him. That night we ended up at the blues again as Lee was a party animal. He hardly seemed to sleep.

  One thing Lee loved to do was have a gossip. I mean that in the nicest possible way. You just couldn't tell him anything in confidence. There were a few times where I had told him something about someone and then later on if we bumped into that person he would repeat what I had said about them to their face. On one occasion I had mentioned to Lee that this kid was a grass. Later that day we saw the lad in 'Boro and Lee went up to him and say, "Oi you're a grass." The kid of course denied it so Lee turned to me and said "Didn't you say he was a grass Bri?" Of course I had and the lad was, but it didn't stop me going red with embarrassment.

  Lee had a lot of good qualities and one of them was admitting when he was wrong. Like most people he could argue till he was blue in the face but if he was proved wrong then he would always apologise and admit that he was wrong. His pet hates were police informers and nonces. He hated them both in equal measure. He knew who all the local informers were and let me know their names which was a big help to me. Lee kept taxing six lads on a regular basis and they were all drug dealers from Redcar, Eston and Teesville. The six of them all sold the gear together like a little firm. One day I asked Lee why he kept taxing these same dealers. Lee told me that all of them worked as police informers. "Why do you think they never go to jail Bri? Because they put everyone in jail who's around them!" I would never have thought the lads Lee was talking about were like that because they made out that they were gangsters and followed the criminal code of honour. A few years later there was a huge case involving over 20 dealers in 'Boro and all of those informers names appeared in the local newspaper, so his information was good. As for nonces he wouldn't think twice about knocking one of them out. He was inside with my good friend Charles Salvador and he has spoken to Steve Wraith about the day he used one nonce as punch bag in the prison gym half killing him. It was the least he deserved. Those people make me physically sick.

  Lee did have regrets in life. He loved his Mam dearly and he was ashamed of what he had put his Mother through over the years. If he could have turned the clock back he would have changed that. His Mam stuck by him through thick and thin and she never let him down with visits or letters and he appreciated that.

  Lee was very loyal to his friends as any of those close to him will tell you. If you had his back then he would have yours, but if you wronged him he would never forget it. Tony Johns and Lee both told me a story on separate occasions which gives a good example of Lee's loyalty. Lee was out in the Commercial pub in Southbank and was on his own. There were five or six other lads in there, full of drink and getting mouthy and Lee knew something was going to kick off. Tony Johns from Grangetown and another lad called 'Maggot' walked in and said hello to Lee. He told them that he thought that he was going to have a bit 'chew' with the other lads in the bar. Tony looked over at them and agreed and told Lee not to worry as they had his back and he and 'Maggot' started walking over to confront the lads. Seeing that Lee now had back up the lads clearly didn't fancy it and ran out of the door and up the street. Lee shook Tony and 'Maggot's' hands and thanked them both and said, "If you ever need me I will always be there for the both of you." And he meant it.

    Lee's first taste of the night life in 'Boro had been as a young lad working as a glass collector in a pub in Middlesbrough. At this pub there was a lad who worked on the door called 'Ducko' who Lee looked up to. Lee even got his hair cut the same as 'Ducko' and he would always hang around the door to speak with him when it was quiet. 'Ducko' was well known and could have a fight. Despite being younger than 'Ducko' and the other door lads he was good crack and the lads all took to him. Lee was a big lad for his age and was full of fun and would make the lads laugh with his comments and sense of humour. On a night off the door team would drink in the Fountain pub in Ormesby and one Saturday afternoon they were all in there letting their hair down when Lee turns up on a motorbike with no helmet on. He came into the pub and was followed by the police a couple of minutes later asking where the lad was who had been riding the stolen bike. The door lads said that they hadn't seen anybody come in and carried on with their conversation. The police having drawn a blank left. Lee thanked the lads for covering for him and a stronger bond was formed.

    As Lee got older and stronger he was determined to get to the top of the 'fighting' tree so he started fighting people with reputations. He had loads of bottle and confidence and would often walk into pubs and clubs on his own and challenge the hardest men there. In those days doormen were doormen and you had to be able to fight, unlike now. These days they have radios to the police if it kicks off. In our day there was a lot of people who could fight for fun. So if someone came to a door and offered you out you would have to fight them. If you didn't fight him then you would never live it down and you would get sacked. Scores were settled with fists like proper men. Not like today where they jump you in numbers or use a knife.

    I think Lee's biggest asset other than his obvious strength, speed and accuracy was that he didn't have any fear. He would fight one or ten at the same time, it did not matter to him. The longer the odds the more he seemed to like it. He loved the challenge. Reputations didn't concern Lee either. When he was inside he owed a local 'face' a few quid . This man fancied himself as a bit of a gangster but Lee was in jail and had said he was going to sort it upon his release. With a week to go Lee got an extra fourteen days added to his sentence for a daft scuffle on the landing. The man who Lee owed the money to was unaware of the situation and annoyed that Lee had not come to see him to repay the money he turned up at Lee's girlfriends door and made the fatal mistake of screaming and shouting at Lee's girlfriend asking where his money was. She tried to explain to him that Lee hadn't been released but the lad carried on demanding the money. So when she went to see Lee on a visit she told him what had happened and that the man had scared her. Lee was raging when he heard this and on the day of his release he went straight to the man's house and banged on his door and told him to get out- side. The man, give him his due, was game and came straight outside but Lee caught him straight away and put him down. Lee told him to get back up which he did and Lee put him down again. The lad was no mug and got up again but for the third time was lying horizontally in his flower beds. He got up for a fourth time but another flooring was all he could take and he told Lee he was done.

Lee told him to never go to his door and speak to his girl like that again. The message was received loud and clear. Lee never forget what this lad had done and he 'taxed' him for £500 on a couple of occasions too, just to remind him that if you crossed the 'Duffer' he didn't forget.

As I have already said reputations meant nothing to Lee. There was a top drug dealer from 'Boro who was also a boxer and had won an ABA title. Lee went to his house with Craig Howard in the car and beeped the horn outside his house. The lad came out of the house, all 18 stone of him and said "What's up?" Lee replied, "Get back in that house and get me an ounce of coke and a grand or I will get out of this car and come in there and take the fucking lot off ya and then Im gonna knock you out." The lad went back in the house and came out minutes later with what Lee had asked for.

Lee's loyalty shone through when I had a rick with a doorman in Redcar. I had been out with Emma and had a nice night and we had decided to call into 'Silks Niteclub' which was on Redcar sea front. When we got to the door 'Dawsey' a really overweight doorman, as tall as he was wide, said to me, "You can't come in with trackies on." I had a feeling I might have trouble getting in as the new owner of the club didn't like me so I knocked the doorman clean out in the foyer and continued to walk in with Emma. Emma being Emma said, "Let's just leave it Brian as two more doorman approached me. I knocked them out as well I clocked another two running from the back of the club and as they got towards me I grabbed both of them and banged their heads together. Another doorman who worked at another club was in there drinking not working and decided to intervene and tried to grab me so I hit him with a peach of a shot right on the money and he was totally unconcious. It was time to leave. I didn't like the place anyway. We headed back to Emma's that night and the following day Lee picked me up and we called to see another mate who is sadly no longer with us called 'Chino'.

'Chino' had been in the club the night before and had seen the whole thing. He told me when the off duty doorman had come round he was shouting his mouth off in the club saying he was going to beat me up and that I had hit him slyly, which was rubbish. I was fuming! It turned out that he lived two minutes from his house so Lee and I decided to drive round. We pulled up at the house and went to the door and the lad opened it. When he saw me he tried to turn and run towards the back door but I grabbed him and threw him around like a ragdoll. As I was hitting him Lee said, "I think he's had enough Bri. I think he could die if you hit him anymore!" I listened to what Lee was saying and stopped and fair play to the lad. He never went to the police and instead approached me a few weeks later in 'Sharky's' in Redcar and apologised. He said that he deserved it for shouting his mouth off and that he had been full of drink. I told him to forget it and shook his hand.

I was in 'Sharkeys' again the following night this time with Emma when I was approached by a man wearing motorbike leathers and a crash helmet. He walked right up to me and lifted his visor and said to me that if he had been on the door the other night that 'shit' wouldn't of happened and I wouldn't have got in. It was then that I realised this was another doorman from 'Silks' where I had been fighting. I couldn't believe what I was hearing so I slapped him...well his helmet and just saw his head hit both sides of the inside of his helmet before he fell to the floor in slow motion. He was out for the count so we decided to leave.

Looking back now I feel sorry for Emma. We never seemed to have a night out without someone having a pop at me. Even going out for a meal had its issues. I had decided to take Emma for a parmo in "Bibis" in Redcar. We never even got to sit down before someone was putting it on my toes. I ended up punching the lad but two of his mates joined in. So I was now in the street fighting three of them. The three of them ended up laid out in the street. It was a good job Emma only lived a minute away from there as the police turned up but we were well gone and we never got our parmo.

Emma was used to the chaos. She had left home at a young age when her mother died and she had a little bedsit opposite the cinema in Redcar when I had met her. Her landlord was always picking on her and giving her a hard time. After the incident at 'Bibis' we had headed back to the bedsit and I had stayed there. Her landlord lived on the premises at that time and the next morning he was banging on her door. She opened the door and he was shouting at her and complaining about her slamming a door when we had come in the previous night. This guy was a bully and always off his head on speed and was getting more aggressive so I jumped out of bed and went to the landing where he was giving Emma a hard time and said, "Who the fuck do you think you're talking to?" He went to answer but I was that mad he was speaking to her like that I ended up kicking him from the top of the stairs to the bottom. It's funny looking back on it now, but he had the last laugh at the time because when she next went out he changed the locks and wouldn't let her back in and refused to give her belongings to her. At the time Emma was too scared to tell me as she knew what I would do and she had to accept it and move on and start again. She eventually told me years later.

Chapter Thirteen: Living Like Kings

Teaming up with Lee had been the right thing to do. When we were together nobody and I mean nobody tried to attack or kill either of us, and when we were together we knew that we had each others backs. To be honest we lived like kings. We went to pubs, nightclubs, restaurants and we never paid. Taxi drivers would never ask for money and we got meals and drinks for free. We weren't 'taxing' these people they just gave us stuff for free. It wasn't just in 'Boro either it was all over Teesside. Designer clothes shops were only too happy to sort us out to although one man at a shop called 'Tin Pan Alley' was telling anyone that would listen that if me and Duffy went to his shop that we would be getting 'fuck all.' Well if that wasn't an invitation! Lee and I visited his two shops. I took over thirty pairs of jeans whilst Lee grabbed all the shirts and tops. Needless to say the people in the shop didn't try to stop us. We took all the stuff to another well known designer shop in 'Boro and sold the clothes to him for £2k. Not a bad days work all round.

One Saturday afternoon Lee wanted to call into the 'Masham' which was a pub in Middlesbrough centre that was always busy on a Saturday afternoon with dealers. As we got to the door Lee asked me to watch his back. Lee knew everyone in there and as I sat on a table Lee stood up and summoned people over and told them to empty what they had on the table. One by one they would hand over their money and drugs. All the ones Lee called over were either grasses or worked for grasses. This was Lee's way of humiliating them. On some occasions I would tell Lee that he had missed a certain dealer and he would tell me that he was okay as he wasn't an informer. Lee always did his homework.

Lee would also like to go to these dealers houses in Boro. He would go in and sit down and say, "Have you got owt for me?" Meaning any information on drug dealers who were due a delivery or anyone who had a stash house or had an amount of money. They would rather give Lee the information and get a wage then be 'taxed' themselves. It was an effective and profitable way of making money. We were always one step ahead of the local dealers as we had friends in places such as Leeds, Liverpool and Manchester who would tip us off on any local deliveries in exchange for a good wage. We had the place sewn up. On one occasion we went to a lad's house called 'Bam Bam.' We knocked on the door but he had gone out the back door as we were walking up the path. His girlfriend opened the door and explained that he was 'shitting himself.' We decided to leave him. We weren't totally ruthless. Only when we needed to be.

A few weeks later Lee pulled up at 'Park End Post Office.' It was giro day. Lee waited until certain dealers arrived and one by one he 'taxed' their giros. These weren't nice people. They were all scumbags, people who wouldn't think twice about robbing you or your family. Take the Grove Hill lads for instance. They were all carrying knifes and up to all sorts. Lee rounded them all up and took everything off them. Drugs, money, mobiles everything and none of them did anything to stop him. They were cowards and petrified of him. There is no doubt in my mind that we were Teeside drug dealers worst nightmare.

One day me and Lee were in a street called Parliament Road in Middlesbrough. We had just left the Chinese, where we'd had some food. Two detectives stopped us and told us that they were receiving over one hundred calls a day about us across the region about our activities. He went on to say that only ten per cent of the calls were true but that the stuff we were doing was crazy and that it was only going to end in one of two ways for us both. We would end up doing life or dying. He finished off by saying that we were 'terrorising Teeside.' I explained to him that were only terrorising, drug dealers, and scumbags and that we weren't terrorising normal people. Lee then said, "We're policing the area better than you. I bet your jobs are easier with us about." One of the detectives shook his head and told us to think about what he had said and then they walked off. Looking back on that conversation now the detective who said this to us was a hundred per cent right, but at that time our attitude was 'If we die, we die. If we get jail, we do the time.' We thought we were invincible and we thought it would last forever, but as you know nothing lasts forever.

Lee and I had to change tactics again. As I have already said it doesn't take long for word to get around, especially in Middlesbrough and especially where me and Lee were concerned. We worked out that a Saturday afternoon would be the best day to hit the dealers as people would buy what they needed on a Friday and make it all into deals for the Saturday. Saturday was the main night for the 'Havana' and club scene in Middlesbrough. People would get their deals ready and go out early on a Saturday in the pubs and sell it through the day. We tried going out at midday for a couple of weeks but we drew a blank so we gave it a go at teatime. In those days a lot of well paid workers like scaffolders who loved going on an all day bender would use Saturday for a 'blacken' which means finishing work before dinner or earlier and going on a pub crawl during the day. By teatime they would need a 'livener,' to pick themselves up. Students would sort out their fix too just before thy headed out so 'taxing' at teatime made perfect sense to me. So we started hitting known places at tea time.

Lee would take one door and I would take the other scanning the whole place. What we tended to find was if we went to tax say a blow dealer on a Saturday afternoon there would be one person selling 'E's' another selling speed, another maybe acid. So when we grabbed the one selling weed he would say "Please don't, I will show you who's selling the E's or the speed." That meant more money for us as ecstasy was selling on the streets for twenty quid a tablet and speed was a tenner a wrap. So we would tax all the pub dealers and then we would hit the hard core 'E' dealers in the clubs. You would always find them in the toilets. We would usually send a young lad to go and buy a few off different people. In those days there was not a lot of CCTV in the clubs and definitely none in the toilets so they felt safe in there. The dealers would usually have all their gear in one pocket and all the money in another. You would get some idiots who used to have a bum bag with the full lot in. The ones who were selling it were all taking it usually and there would be no dramas taking it off them. A bit like taking candy off a baby.

The clubs were always packed. They were always dark with strobe lights flashing, deafening music and smoke machines, which helped us go about our business unnoticed. We started making a lot of money on Saturday night in Middlesbrough alone. A lot more than when we were just taxing weed dealers. As well as using a young girl to locate the dealers we would bung the doormen a few quid to tip us off too. We couldn't lose really.

We were still 'taxing' during the day too. We got a tip off from a lad called 'Flea' that a dealer was getting 4 kilos of weed dropped off. 'Flea' used to sell weed and was going to get a drink out of it so decided to tell us so he could get a bigger piece of the pie. Faily and Shaun were with us that day but wanted nothing to do with it as they knew the dealer, but Lee and I had no allegiance to him so we were game. We offered 'Flea' a kilo in exchange for the tip off and to help us plan a way to tax the dealer without him suspecting 'Flea.' We decided the best way to do it would be when the drop was happening. The plan worked like clockwork. As soon as the lad dropped it at 'Fleas' we barged 'Flea's' door to grab the gear. The lad who had dropped the gear saw all this but was too scared to stop his car as he probably had more gear and cash in his motor. "Flea' then phoned the lad whilst we were there to tell him that the gear was gone and that he had been ragged all over. The dealer took it all in and put it down to experience. 'Flea' was over the moon because he had scored for a kilo and we were well happy with how well our plan had worked. So why fix something that isn't broken?

We started doing a few 'taxes' with 'Flea' because he knew everyone in Middlesbrough and he was a really good lad. I remember one we did in Whinney Banks, Middlesbrough. We ordered some stuff off someone and then we got a lad to come down from out of the area who agreed to put ten grand in the pot. We pretended we had ten grand as well, but we only had cut up newspaper as our ten grand which was wrapped in a carrier bag. The lad passed us the real ten grand and 'Flea' took the money to get the 'blow'. Then I got a call off 'Flea' to say the lad who he had gone to meet with the cash had took the cash and driven off. I pretended to be angry at him telling him it was all his fault and telling him to get back now. The lad who had put the ten grand was listening to all of this and when I hung up on 'Flea' I turned to him and said come with me we need to go and sort this out. The lad was shitting himself and wanted no part of it and told us to sort it out ourselves. We never saw or heard from him again and scored for ten grand which we split three ways. That was too easy.

On another occasion 'Flea' rang and said someone was after ten kilos of 'blow'. It was a lad from Stockton called Gary, who I'd had a run in with before I had fought Lee. That was the fight where I broke my finger. He had come in the club with three mates and tried it on. I knocked his three mates out and broke his jaw. So I had no qualms about doing this job. I drove over to see 'Flea' to plan things with him. The lad wanted to test the gear first so we got one good 'bar' as they were called in them days and filled the rest of a big kit bag with bags of sugar. 'Flea' arranged a meet and as the buyers car pulled up he pulled the good 'bar' out and handed it to him through his car window for him to burn. He was impressed and said he would take it. 'Flea' asked him for the money which he duly handed over. 'Flea' passed the bag of sugar over and started his engine. Just before he pulled away 'Flea' said, "Brian Cockerill says thank you very much!" The lad did try to get his money back and tried to get a former boxer from Hartlepool to intervene but he didn't want to get involved.

Another one we did was in Hartlepool with 'Flea' again. The lad we taxed is dead now and was called Ronnie. We got a tip off that he was selling over there so we went over and grabbed him. It turned out that he was selling Ecstasy in a big way. He only had a few hundred quid and about twenty 'E's' on him so I grabbed him by the throat and I said, "Where's the stash?" He told me that he was getting 7,000 dropped off the following day from a guy called 'Cockney Mark'. Happy with this information I calmed down and let him go and told him to ring me when they were coming. We were waiting around the corner in a friend's house the next day when the call finally came. The pills had arrived. We went straight to Ronnie's door and banged on it. He answered and we threw him about a bit to make it look realistic. This fat lad appeared and I asked him his name. Mark, he replied, so I hit him with a right and dropped him and he fell on the settee. He didn't even try to get back up. There was another lad too who tried to jump in so I hit him and dropped him too. There were two more lads there but they didn't want any trouble. I told them not to move and asked them where the gear was. They pointed to a bag on the table. 7,000 pills all present and correct. What a result. We split the spoils between us as always and we gave Ronnie 500 for his troubles. He was delighted and was another one on the Cockerill Duffy payroll after that.

I was talking to Lee Duffy and Lee Harrison one day and they told me a story about the day that they had found out that someone from Liverpool was dropping some 'E's' off for someone at Middlesbrough Station. They were tipped off by a lad from 'Boro and decided to head over to the station that day. Sure enough the lad in question was on the platform waiting for a train coming from Liverpool. The train was on time as Duffy watched the lad from 'Boro approach the carriage of the now stationary train. A man got off the train, greeted the lad and handed over a bag and that's when Duffy pounced and nabbed the bag which had 5,000 'E's' inside. Lee managed to sell them on for £25k leaving the lads from 'Boro and Liverpool with questions to answer and debts to pay. Later that day Lee walked into a known dealers pub and asked for some coke and he put the brief case on the table with the 25 grand in and everyone in the pub saw it and thought Lee was big time. They didn't end up buying drugs they ended up going abroad with it.

Lee and I both enjoyed the gym, as you know, and we trained quite a few times in the short time that we were together. Lee used to 'buzz' when I used to go heavy, whether it be legs or arms. One day we did our legs and Lee started off with 60 kilos of squats for ten. Lee then went to 80 kilos for eight reps. Then he did 100 kilos for six reps. He finished with 120 kilos for few reps and I gave him a couple of touches. Then I started with 140 kilos for ten reps, then 180 kilos for eight reps, 220 kilos for six reps, 260 kilos for four reps, 300 kilos for two reps, 340 kilos for 1 rep and finally 365 kilos for 1 rep. Lee couldn't believe it. He said I've just seen you do that again and I still don't believe it. With Lee having big long legs and big long arms it was good for boxing but not good for bench pressing etc. Lee wasn't natural either. He had been taking steroids since our fight after Craig told him that he needed to get bigger to fight. Lee was taking more steroids to combat the weight he was losing due to the drugs but I will go into that later in this book.

We didn't do every job for money. Stuey Stamp was a good friend of mine and Lee. His son Phil Stamp played football for 'Boro and England. Stuey used to have the 'Market Tavern' in North Ormesby in Middlesbrough. Another good pal of mine lived there called Muzza. So one day I got a call off 'Stampy' saying this lad had started coming into his pub who had just finished a 12 stretch and was making a nuisance of himself. This lad was known to carry knives and guns and people were scared of him and 'Stampy' was starting to lose customers because of him. He was starting fights with young lads and taking liberties with pensioners too. I hated bullies and this guy needed teaching a lesson. I made a few calls and me and the lads jumped in the car to go and find this lad. We just missed him at the pub but 'Stampy' had got his address for me. We went round to his house and were braying on the door but there was no answer. His neighbour came out and said that he hadn't seen him for a week or so. It turned out that he had been tipped off that I was looking for him so had headed back to Darlington and was never seen again. 'Stampys' pub went from strength to strength after that.

I helped him again when he was getting problems from a well known figure from Park End. 'Stampy' rang me and told me that there was a whole crew of lads going in from the local estate and causing trouble. They were bullying and scaring people. So me, Peter Robbo and Tony Johns went in and they clocked us straight away and all ran out of the pub. 'Stampy' came straight over to us and thanked us. He knew the sight of us walking in would be enough to scare them away. He offered to pay us but we told him not to be daft. He was a good mate. He had a bit of grief with the same lads again when I was in the 'Theatre.' This time it was two of the main lads who were giving him a hard time. He had managed to get a message to me so I headed up to the bar and walked in at closing time. They were shouting and bawling at 'Stampy' so I shouted across the bar at them, "Come and bully me." They both turned white and put their hands up in the air and said simultaneously, "No Brian, we want no trouble with you." I told them in no uncertain terms that if they had trouble with 'Stampy' then they had trouble with me. They rather sheepishly apologised and went on their way. They never bothered 'Stampy' again.

Chapter Fourteen: A Speedy Game Of Cat And Mouse

One day I got a visiting order to go and see a pal in prison called 'Speedy'. The first time I met Speedy was when I was working the doors for John Black. Speedy was a kickboxer who was taught by Paul Sexton. John Black had a fight one night and the lads who he was scrapping with got him locked up and they made a statement against him. I heard about this the next day so I went round to 'Speedy's' house, who I was told knew the lad involved, and asked him to contact the lad that had pressed charges. 'Speedy' said he would do one better than that and would take me to the lad's house. I asked the lad why he had pressed charges when it was him that caused the trouble in the first place. The sight of me and 'Speedy' in his living room was enough to get him to withdraw his statement. That was my first meeting with 'Speedy' and we kept in touch after that.

Lee and Craig Howard decided to come with me on this visit. We got to the prison and when we arrived in the visiting room Lee lit a joint up. I said, "Lee what you doing? There's screws there." Lee laughed and replied, "Fuck them!" He walked right up to one of the screws and inhaled the joint and blew it right in his face. The screw said nothing. It was clear he didn't want any trouble. When you go on a visit you're meant to sit at designated table with who you've gone to see and stay at that table and not walk around. Not Lee though. He got up from the table and walked to one table, and then another, and then another, talking to different prisoners he knew. One of the screws went to say something but the other screw nudged him and shook his head as if to say leave him. Lee didn't give a fuck.

He had met 'Speedy' a couple of times through me when we were over in Stockton taxing as 'Speedy' knew every drug dealer in Stockton and Billingham and he was feared in the area as he was known for stabbing people and he also had access to guns. He was given misleading information once from an ex girlfriend who had told him that her boyfriend who she was with at the time had been hitting their daughter that she had previously with 'Speedy'. He found out about this and went straight to the house to sort this man out. He was off his head and stabbed the boyfriend in the eye and blinded the lad and was now serving time for that attack.

I'd had trouble with the same lad in the past as he was part of the notorious 'wrecking crew,' who were a gang of twenty lads or so that used to go round the pubs in Stockton terrifying the doorman. They would empty fruit machines and help themselves to drinks behind the bar. It turned out that the lad who 'Speedy' had blinded hadn't done anything to 'Speedy's' daughter. It had all been lies from his ex just to cause trouble which had resulted in one being blinded and the other lad being jailed.

Lee and 'Speedy' clashed before Lee's death when I was in prison. Lee had 'taxed' two of 'Speedy's' dealers in Stockton. Speedy always carried a knife but when he heard what had happened he got tooled up with a gun and was telling everyone that he was going to 'fucking shoot Duffy.' He kept his wits about him as he knew Duffy would be looking for him and was lying low in Garby with a few mates. He was waiting for Duffy to make his move and 'tax' a few lads there. Once he made his move he planned on shooting him.

Lee found out what was happening and got a couple of cars full of lads together and got a lad from Thornaby called Jimmy to go with them as he knew 'Speedy's' whereabouts. At the time Speedy was driving a XRI. Duffy started kicking doors in all over Stockton trying to find him. Lee was started to get agitated so grabbed one lad and in total fear when asked where 'Speedy' was said, "I've just seen him in his car in Roseworth outside Aki the taxi drivers house." Aki's real name was Andrew Atkinson. So Lee jumped in his car and flew straight over with Jimmy who showed him the house. Aki was stood outside as they arrived. Lee said, "Where's Speedy?" Aki said, "I don't know." Lee wasn't convinced and called him a liar explaining that someone had told him that 'Speedy's' car had just been seen parked up outside his house. Aki insisted that he hadn't seen him. Aki and Speedy went back a long way and Aki wasn't going to give him up that easy. Aki was a mixed martial arts expert, who had trained kids who'd become champions. He also worked the doors and was frightened of no man. He was one of the most genuine men I knew but he stood no chance against eight lads tooled up. He was concerned too as his six week old baby was next to him in a pram. Lee was off his head and told Aki to get in his car. Aki refused so Lee told him again to get in the car. Aki wasn't having it. So Lee went to pick the baby up from the pram and said "If you won't come then we will take your baby." That was not going to happen so Aki had no choice but to get in the car and go looking for 'Speedy.'

As they were driving around, Aki just kept giving them false information and wrong addresses to protect his friend. He tried to keep them calm and at one point started talking about fishing and anything else just to keep the situation at ease. They couldn't find 'Speedy' and finally dropped Aki off at home. Later that night Jimmy who had shown Duffy Akis house was working the door in Stockton. 'Speedy' turned up with Aki and asked him if he could have a word with him outside. Aki beat Jimmy up badly and rightly so. Jimmy told them that he didn't have a choice as Duffy had just turned up at his door but it fell on deaf ears. I have to be honest here and say that when I heard that Lee had threatened to take the baby it really annoyed me. Aki was a good friend to me and no matter what happened between them he should not have involved the baby. Threatening women and kids is a strict no no in my book. 'Speedy' went to ground again after that leaving Lee even more frustrated.

Not all taxes went to plan with Lee. I remember one where we went looking for a lad who was selling drugs, his name escapes me so let's call him Tommy. Anyway we went to the door and knocked on it and asked if Tommy lived there. The lad who answered said he did but that he was out at that moment. He then asked if we wanted to leave a message. I said no and asked where he had gone and what time would he be back? The lad who was being very helpful pointed to the shop at the end of the road. So Lee and I headed to the shop and waited outside. We waited for what seemed like ages before heading back to the house and knocking again. A different person answered this time explaining that we had just missed Tommy. Turns out it was him that I had been talking to in the first place. Smart kid had blagged us. You learn by your mistakes. After that we always took someone who could identify the dealer.

  Going back to 'Flea', I'd just been round to his house to see him. When I left, the drug squad pulled up outside his house with the armed police. 'Flea' said they were shouting "Armed police" and running into his house before they arrested him and his lass. They then started searching the house from top to bottom. They found what they were looking for in a little cupboard in the kitchen under the stairs. It was a big bag of white powder. One of the cops put his finger in lightly and put his finger to his mouth and went, "Aarrrrggghhh" it was artex! Despite an intensive search they drew a blank and as 'Flea' and his partner were released he rubbed their noses in it.

  Another 'tax 'Lee and I did was in Middlesbrough. A lad had ordered seven kilos of 'blow'. So we went to the house where the deal was going down and we hid in the back of the house. When the lad arrived we came into the front room and took the seven kilo of 'blow' off him. All of a sudden there was a power cut in the full street and the lad whose stuff it was made a grab for the bag and tried to get out the door. Obviously we got it in the end but it was a fucking nightmare as we couldn't see a thing. We got the seven kilos and gave the lad who set it up and whose house it was one kilo and me and Lee kept three each.

  On another occasion Lee knew someone from Bradford who got in touch and said that he had some 'bits and bobs' if he could sell any. Lee said he could and ordered half a kilo of coke. We had to wait a few days till it got sorted out and we arranged to meet them at a church near the 'Bluebell.' On the way there we decided that we were going to 'tax' the lads instead. The two Asian lads from Bradford arrived and Lee asked if he could test the stuff. The lads agreed so we both got in the car. I grabbed one of the lads in a headlock whilst Lee grabbed the gear. We took their mobiles off them and £220 that they had on them and sent them on their way.

  Thinking back we had some great touches like that. Another we did was in Darlington. The lad used to sell steroids and recreational. So me and Lee planned it all out. We got a lift off a lad from Southbank and we got to the lad's house. This lad had a top of the range Porsche where he kept the gear. We got him to open the boot and we took all the steroids and stuff out of the back. We got about five grands worth of steroids and Craig Howard sold the lot to a bodybuilder in Bradford. Craig said he sold them for three grand so that's what Lee and I got. Craig probably sold them for more but we were happy with the three grand.

We went to another house in Darlington to tax a lad whose girlfriend worked for the dole. We got to this big posh house with big black gates. I said I would kick the door in as his Mrs was at work. We went up the steps and a woman came out and said, "What do you's want?" I was a bit shocked as I didn't expect to see a woman so I asked her if Steve was in. She told me that he was out and wondered if she could help. She then told me that she was a Crown Court Judge. It was clear that he was inside and had sent her outside to try and get rid of us. We decided it wasn't worth the hassle and I didn't like the fact that there was a woman there anyway. As we were coming away from Darlington a police car started to follow us. Then the blue lights went on. We were lucky that we had a good driver that day who managed to out run the police and eventually lose them. It was just another sticky situation where we could have got caught. It was never ending. Day after day we were taxing. We would carry on through the night sometimes. It could be two in the morning or eight in the morning we were taxing people all hours.

I remember the day when Lee wanted to have a run up to Dickie Dido's, from Stokesley. When we got there he was with old Tom Petch. Dickie and Tom used to go rabbiting with the dogs and a lamp. We went to a few pubs up there and we were all having a good laugh. They were telling us all their stories and making us laugh. As the drinks flowed Duffy was doing his one legged squats and they had me doing my party piece yet again, dead lifting cars. Lee could also do one armed push ups. He could get about 100 reps with one arm. We stayed up their until teatime and got some food in the pub before heading back to 'Boro. We had a couple of drinks before going to Belmont to see our mate Freddie. We had all dropped a few ecstasy and were having fun and dancing about. We hooked up with John Graham and Terry Dicko and decided to go to Bryan Andrew's place the 'Havana.'

When the club shut at 2am we headed to the blues. Lee was shaddow boxing and taking his shirt off and posing. He would always be doing mad things. This night he was telling me jokes and making me laugh and he grabbed me and cuddled me and said "I love you." The E's were kicking In. When we had E's Lee would always be dead loving and would always say "I would give my life for you and I know you would for me." We had a really good bond. That night always stays in my mind. No trouble, just frisk, fun and lots of laughs. That was also the last time I saw Lee Duffy.

Lee would love winding people up. He would say this is the lad that wants to fight you Bri and bring some poor bloke over and watch his reaction. Terry Dicko still does that to me to this day. I would always get a bit embarrassed and not know what to say when Lee did this whilst he was laughing behind the poor lad's back. The time we spent together was full of these situations and not violence. I rarely saw Lee punch anybody.

Lee did enjoy fighting, of that there is no doubt. He liked a challenge. It used to frustrate him that so many of his fights were so easy. We all get days when we are down and depressed but I never saw Lee like that. He always had a spring in his step and was one of those people always on the move. He never stayed anywhere for too long and was always full of energy.

Sometimes Lee would go missing for a few days to see Stephen and Michael Sayers in Newcastle. Or he would be up and down the country meeting people that he had been in jail with. He had many stints in prison, and when you add it all up Lee was only on the streets for a few years. I have read one author's account that says Lee ran 'Boro for 12 years. That is totally untrue.

The following day I had gone out with some doormen from Grangetown. Tony Stubbs,Tony Johns, Bernie, Ginger Alan and Maggot. We had been over Southbank and we had decided to go to Redcar. I would always bump into Emma in Redcar but she never came out that day. We went on a pub crawl and I was drunk and full of E. I remember I had about three grand on me and I remember taking it out of my pocket and Tony Johns saying, "Bloody hell Bri look at all that money!" I bought everyone in the pub a drink. We were all having a good night. I bumped into little Frankie Atherton and we went into 'Sharkeys', then the 'Hydro.' From there we decided to go down to 'Silks.'

As we headed round the corner we could see the club and one of Lee's friends was on the floor and getting a kicking from the doormen. I got to the door and asked one of the lads what he was doing. He blanked me and was still kicking the kid so I grabbed a hold of him and started to pull him off. Unbeknown to me the police had been watching and were on their way over to the door and grabbed a hold of my arms. As they did this the twenty stone doorman that had been kicking the lad on the ground ran over to me and punched me in the face. I went mad and started screaming and shouting and was arrested. They took me to Guisborough police station and left me in the van for about half an hour to calm down. I was screaming and shouting at them and kicking off. They finally got me out and took me to the desk. They searched me and found the lump of money I had. They made a note of my injuries. My hand was cut and I had a cut on my head where the doorman had hit me when the police had hold of my arms. They then put me in a cell. There was a matress but it was made of wood and it was freezing cold. I didn't sleep well. They came to the cell at 6am and released me. It was a Saturday morning. I was charged with criminal damage to the police vehicle.

I went home, got a shower and then went for a parmo with my mate Mark from Southbank. Lee had gone to Newcastle on the Friday and hadn't returned. After my food I headed over to Emma's for a few hours and Mark agreed to pick me up on his way back from his girlfriends. When Mark picked me up we were passing through Eston and I caught a glimpse of the doorman who was called 'Ste' who had punched me when the police were restraining me in a kebab shop. So Mark pulled over and I went into the kebab shop, which was all camera'd up. As soon as 'Ste' saw me he tried to throw a punch so I hit him first and knocked him clean out. He was taken to hospital. I had broken his jaw. A couple of hours later he had made a statement against me, so the police were looking for me again.

I laid low at Emma's for a few days but was taking E's and feeling paranoid. I kept getting up and walking around and looking out of her window. She kept trying to reassure me that there was nobody outside but I was convinced they were watching me and that Emma's flat would one of the first places they would come. They had just raided Frankie's place amongst others where they had caught me previously so I moved into Mally's flat above Emma and felt a bit more secure. I couldn't hide forever though and I had to go out because I was like a caged lion and they finally nicked me and charged me with assault. The following day I was up in court and I was banged up in Durham jail on remand a few hours later. To say I was shocked was an understatement. With only one charge and one statement against me I should have been on bail. Lee had been up for three or four assaults and got bail, as had others.

When I arrived at the prison I had to have an induction. They carried out the usual searches, gave me some food and then escorted me to the wing where I met up with Elvis Tomo who I was going to sharing a cell with. In prison you have time to think and reflect and I felt as if this was a deliberate ploy by the police to separate me from Lee. Lee always had trouble when we weren't together. He had been shot and shot at over the last few months. When we were together he had no trouble at all.

I had plenty of visits when I was on remand. Mark was a regular as was Craig Howard and they were both keeping me updated on what was going on over the wall. I was disappointed that Lee had not been to see me despite him sending in messages with the lads. I was annoyed at the time but looking back it was due to his intake of drugs and the realisation that his life was spiralling out of control. He had started taking crack cocaine which was causing a lot of his issues and was spending a lot of time on his own. "United you stand. Divided you Fall." as Lee Harrison used to say. Never a truer word spoken. Lee was out of control and was staying up all night.

Lee was losing weight and wasn't training properly. When you're on that shit your mind is all over the place. I should know. I've been there. I cabined myself up when I was on it but Lee was still going out and about and was leaving himself wide open for attack. Some people close to him said that he was out of control and hitting people for no reason. He will have been paranoid. Lee was a good lad and I loved him but the drugs destroyed him like they do to a lot of people.

Every three days in Durham you were supposed to get a video but I seemed to be getting missed out, so I started arguing with one of the screws called Brian Robson. I got nowhere with my complaint and a day later the heavy squad were outside my door all shielded up to move me onto good order and discipline wing. So I was put into segregation but I had company in the cell next door. Elvis Tomo followed was banged up in the seg to for hitting Mcpartland. It meant we got to talk out of the window to each other to pass some time. We used to have to shit and piss in a bucket and slop out. For entertainment we got a book called 'The Magic Cottage.' Elvis read it first then I read it. On the other side of me was a man called Patrick Tapper. I knew Dave and Tony Tapper as they used to work with me and John Black and Bernie Mcdevit on the doors.

He started telling me the story of what had happened between him and Lee Duffy. He told me that he was the person that had thrown petrol on him in a bar. He was sick of hearing Duffy's name been bandied about. Duffy this and Duffy that, he said it was driving him mad. So he approached Lee in a bar and asked him for a fiver. Lee was always giving money to people but on this occasion he didn't have a fiver but gave him £3.50 in change. Tapper was a window cleaner and had a bucket with him so he walked out of the bar to the nearby petrol station and filled it with petrol at the pump. He then went back to the pub and threw the contents of his bucket all over Lee. It was claimed that he tried to light a match but that Lee was too quick for him and started laying into him and rightly so as he had just tried to kill him. Lee was arrested and charged for the incident. Lee spent the next night or so in Newcastle with the Sayers before returning to 'Boro. He took his kids out to the fair on his return and then headed out with his mates. That night Lee Duffy was involved in an altercation and died. I am not going to go into the incident. I wasn't there and it has been well documented and I do not wish to put the family through any more pain.

I was told the news by Tapper on the landing the following day. I was devastated and felt helpless. I was convinced if I had been there that this would never have happened. It made me more convinced that this had all been part of the police plan and why I had been remanded. I put in a request to the governor to go to his funeral which was swiftly rejected as I wasn't a relation. I was gutted. I saw coverage of the funeral in the paper and was so pleased that he got a great turn out. I just wish that I could have been there.

The drugs eventually took over and destroyed me. I lost Emma and my life was spiralling out of control too. Someone told me Emma had died. My true love gone. I felt I had nothing. But someone was watching over me or I got extremely lucky. I managed to find the inner strength to get myself clean and come off drugs. I found Emma was alive and well and we reconnected on Facebook, and last and by no means least I found Jesus in my heart. I just wish Lee could have been with me on this particular journey.

I think if Lee had been here today he would have been with me doing the anti-knife campaign and going into schools and telling kids to stay away from drugs and not to follow in our footsteps. Kids would have listened to him. The biggest run of results I ever had 'taxing' was after Lee's death. I earned quarter of a million pound in a month. Me and a couple of travelling lads arranged to get some lads from Spennymoor who had a big house. We had people watching the house. There was three of them and they had Weimaraner dogs. One of the lads called Tommy, who is dead now had a burger van and they all did cigarettes in large quantities and had numerous other businesses. They were splashing the cash too with the people watching the house seeing various items being delivered including a grand piano.

One of the lads was living near the Bongo in Middlesbrough so we knocked on his door. He was a big lad, tall but skinny. He shit himself straight away and told us that he didn't have any money but we knew he was lying, so we told him to arrange a meet with the other two lads. He agreed and made a call. We met them and I told them that we wanted twenty grand. "What each?" said one of the lads. I'd only meant twenty grand between them but seeing as he had offered, it would be rude to say no. "Yes £20k each." I said. They didn't bat an eyelid and asked for a week to sort the cash out. I told them they could have three days. They didn't get back to me which a bit of a concern at first. Then the call came a week later than agreed and we arranged a meet on the A66 near Mcdonalds. They gave us seventy thousand pounds as I charged them an extra £10k for messing us about. Twenty grand of the cash was in Scottish notes but it all spends!

A week later we got twenty grand off a lad called Charlie from Grove Hill. Some gypsies were 'taxing' him so I stepped in and stopped the 'tax' but I had to give the gypsies a drink. So I gave them ten grand and I got ten grand and everyone was happy. A week later I got another fag man and a week after that another. I had more money than I had ever had in my life. Three quarter of a million pounds. Looking back now I wish I had screwed my loaf on and invested that money.

Chapter 15: Two Speedy Cosworths And A Porsche

We had a tip off about someone in Marske who was selling Ecstasy. We went to the door but to our surprise he opened the door and handed me two hundred 'E's' and a few hundred quid without any drama. From there we went to the house next door where we got another hundred 'E' and a hundred quid. Not bad for ten minutes work. When we got back to 'Boro Lee told everyone that we had took three thousand off them. He loved to exaggerate, but that was Lee's way. He was always laughing and winding people up. I can't remember ever seeing him miserable.

When we used to do jobs with Terry Dixon, Terry loved Lee and they got on really well. Me and Terry would collect debts and never had any sticky situations because we were always polite. We did one for a lad who had a window warehouse. He was owed a hundred and sixty grand and it took about three months to get the money in but we went to every single door until we got it. The only problem is that when you do jobs like that you never know whose door you're knocking on. One of the doors we knocked on this day was a policeman's house. A woman came to the door and I said to her, "You owe five grand." She said, "We are police officers!" Her husband, who was also a copper came out next and I explained that it didn't matter what job they did, they still owed the money, and if they didn't pay it then I'd be taking the conservatory down. After a bit of discussion they told us to come back the next day and they did pay us the money.

Terry and I made a good debt collecting team and with his patter and the sight of me standing at the door we rarely had any problems. We would be happy to negotiate with people to and help them pay what they owed in instalments. It was better doing it diplomatically than having to hit somebody and that way we kept our noses clean and had no issues with the police.

I was offered a job for £10k and offered the work to 'Speedy.' I told him there was no rush and to take his time with it. I didn't bank on him stringing the job out though and that is what he appeared to be doing when I went around to his a month later and he still hadn't got the money in. He said he would get it sorted the following week so seven days later it was the same again from him, "Next week, next week." I was starting to lose my patience. The following week I got a call to say that he had been arrested after his girlfriend had called the police and accused him of assaulting her. The police turned up at her house and there wasn't a mark on her so they explained that they could not take the matter any further. "Well maybe you should take a look in the loft?" She said. The police found three kilos of speed all neatly packed in a box and 'Speedy' was a wanted man. He was duly arrested and received a five year sentence at trial and he still owed me ten grand! I decided to go to see his girlfriend to see what I could of his take to compensate me. She explained to me that he had actually recovered the money and had spent it on a caravan and on a Sierra Cosworth, so I asked her where the car was. She told me that it was over the road at his mates house 'Stevo,' so I went over to see him and he said that the car was in the garage. I told him my situation and that I wanted the car in part payment for the debt. I got no arguments from him and he handed the keys over. I managed to get six grand for the car which meant he still owed me four thousand.

It didn't take 'Speedy' long to find out what I had been doing and a few days later I got a call from him threatening me and telling me that when he got out he was going to shoot me. I told him that I would be waiting for him. A few months later I was arrested for a misdemeanour and was remanded in Durham. 'Speedy' was in a different jail but was sending threats to me as was another inmate Davey Glover. These kind of threats were water off a ducks back to me and I wasn't concerned. The charges against me were dropped and I was released and 'Speedy' was released a short time later. I bumped into him not too long after and he saw me and did a runner. That was the last time I saw him. He tried to 'tax' a dealer in 'Boro a few weeks later but was shot dead and the chances of getting my four grand back went with him.

Lee and I had a good relationship with Craig Howard at first but as time passed by I began to hear stories about him that didn't sit well with me. Firstly I heard that he had been taking cars off a guy in Shipton. One guy was left with nothing as Craig took £100k worth of cars. The man hung himself.

At the time I had a white Cosworth. It was my pride and joy and I had it chipped up to three hundred and thirty brake horsepower. I was in bed one night when I heard a lot of commotion and a car driving off. So I got up and realised that my car was missing. The thieves had been in my house, took two and a half grand in cash and nicked my motor. The 'Tax Man' had been taxed and I was foaming. The next day I was like a mad man going round beating people up trying to get answers. All roads seemed to lead to two lads in Gateshead so I headed up there to see my pal 'Big' Billy Robinson who gave me an address for the 'likely lads.' I got there put the door through only to find out that the lads had been in court that day and had both got five years apiece.

So after hearing the news about my car Craig Howard decided to buy a car identical to the one that I had stolen. My mate Bam Bam said 'He's taking the fucking piss.' He wasn't wrong. I made my mind up to 'tax' him to teach him a lesson. I had previously given Craig a Porsche to sell and I was still waiting for my money from that. He kept avoiding me and putting me off so I decided to head to Bradford to see 'Karad' who was a big time car dealer and who he used to work with. He was a nice guy. When I arrived he was their with two bodyguards but explained that he still had the car and would deal with me direct on it. He then told me that Craig had been telling him that he was 'running' 'Boro and that both Lee and I were his 'soldiers.' He also said that he had offered to fight us both and that were shivering as he spoke to us. Laughable. Armed with this knowledge and proof that my gut instinct about Craig had been right I decided to wait until he got in touch with me.

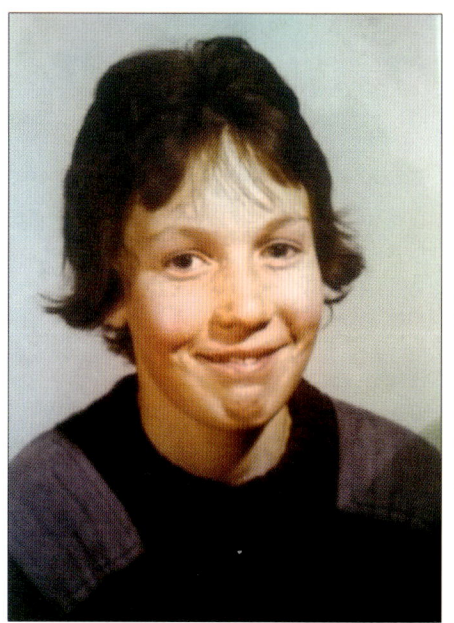

A young Brian Cockerill

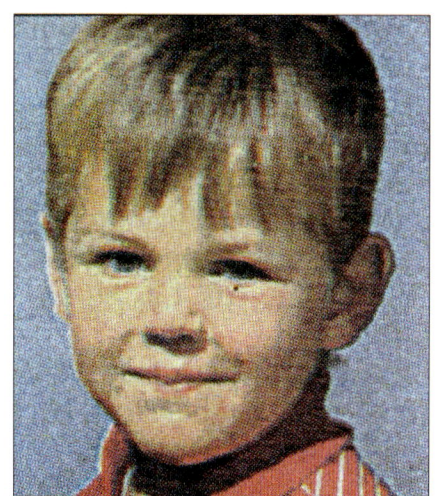

Lee Duffy as a boy

Brian taking part in Mr England

Lee at home in Southbank

Left: Brian at Mr England with his Uncle Frank, who played for Manchester United

Lee and his mam, Brenda on his 21st birthday

Lee wearing the same shirt he had on when he fought Brian

The gentle side of Lee Duffy, holding his daughter

Brian outside Silks Nightclub in Redcar

Big Bri

Big Bri

Lee's handwriting in cards he sent to Carol

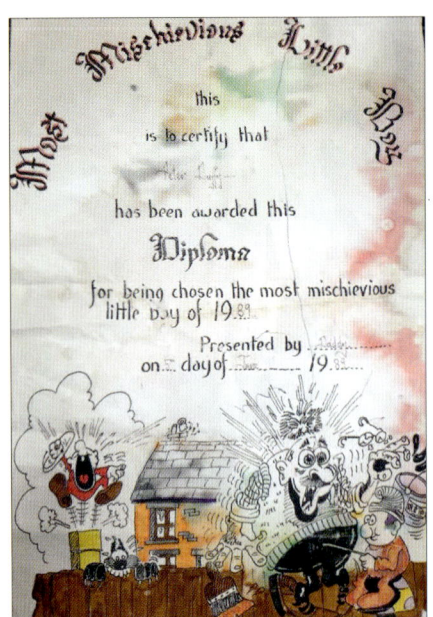

Above: A certificate Lee sent his son, Peter, from Jail

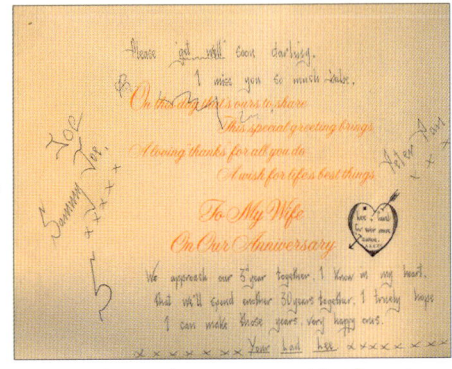

Lee's anniversary card to Carol

Carol with her family

The hardman with a soft centre

CAROL 'Bonnie' Holmstrom probably knew Lee Duffy better than anyone else.

The pair lived as man and wife in South Bank for five years and had two children, Sammy-Jo (now six) and Michelle, four.

Duffy doted on his children and Bonnie's son Peter, from her earlier marriage.

He never cut ties with his children, showering gifts on them. He took the children to Eston Fair the night before he died.

Bonnie first met Lee as 19-year-old, fresh out of jail and full of ideas.

"We hit it off straight away," she said. "He was a well-mannered, polite young man, a bit shy. It took him three weeks to ask me out – at first I said no, but then we went out and had the time of our lives."

Within two months, Duffy was spending most of his time at Bonnie's home in Ann Street, South Bank.

"He told me he loved me forever, which I thought was quite childish. But he flattered me and made me feel wanted. We became part of one another.

"We talked all the time – he was no Bungalow Bill. I spent five years with him and he was not ignorant. He had beautiful handwriting, it was like italic. He always spoke from the heart and expressed himself well in letters.

"He also gave me strength. I was naive when I met Lee and he taught me a lot."

Bonnie, now 30, had never known violence before she met Duffy and although much of his life was shielded from her, she knew what he did – and understood why.

"His background meant he had to be top dog. He knew he had to be big and strong to get on and fought constantly – but it wasn't always Lee that went looking for it. I knew what he was – and respected him for it.

"When his life was done, I was his base – I gave the tender loving care he needed. I'd never paint Lee as whiter than white because he wasn't.

"But I saw another side to him. I loved Lee the hell of a nice lad – not Lee Duffy the reputation. When I met him, no-one knew the name Lee Duffy."

Duffy wanted a home and family and was delighted when Bonnie fell pregnant with Sammy-Jo – his pride and joy.

"We always talked about marriage and the future. I didn't care if we were married or not – I loved him, he loved me and that was it."

But the good times with Lee were tempered by the bad – the angry, violent rows and prison sentences.

After just nine months, Duffy was back in custody – and over the next four years, Bonnie travelled the country to visit him as he bounced in and out of jail.

Duffy was cut over Christmas 1987, when Bonnie fell pregnant again – this time unplanned. But in March he was jailed for four years for his part in a fight at the Spookeasy club (later the Havana) in Linthorpe Road, Middlesbrough.

Things went from bad to worse, Bonnie recalled: "It was starting to show on me. I felt pressurised by Lee's letters, I was drawn and underweight and had little money." In August, Michelle was born prematurely and battled for life. Her heart stopped beating and she almost died during a prison visit.

Bonnie remembers the period as 'doom and gloom' and finally told Lee it was over.

"We couldn't keep expecting loyalty – he was keeping me in a prison, too."

Duffy left prison in May, 1990 and visited Bonnie – who had suffered a breakdown – in hospital. "He cried, then went off on holiday," she said. "He came back and told me Lisa was pregnant. I was numb."

Lee had been involved with Lisa Stockell years before and she had begun visiting him after the relationship with Bonnie ended.

Yet Duffy was never refused entry to Bonnie's home, now in Shinwell Crescent, South Bank. She said: "He was using lots of drugs and would come to recuperate – he would sleep, then spend time with the kids, bathing and playing with them. We would talk about the old times.

"When I was told he had died, I sat down and hardly moved for three days. Then I went through all the emotions, including guilt.

"What I miss most is someone knowing me so well, someone who can look at me and tell what's up. He was my whole world and my world stood still when he died – but my memories bring him alive again.

"My tribute to him was 'No words to say'. I know what I know. Never a day goes by without his name being mentioned in this house. I love him each day and I'm so sad he's gone."

Two other women in Duffy's life claim the good side to his character has been ignored in favour of malicious rumours.

"If I have one memory, it's of how much love he had to give," said his mother Brenda.

Lisa Stockell, mother of Katie Leigh, two years old on February 6, said: "He loved the baby, he bathed her, dressed her, changed her and cared for her. He was a normal, loving father.

"We were ready to settle down. We had a council house in Whale Hill and Lee was decorating it. We even slept there two days before he died – it was empty, but he wanted to stay there."

> 'He loved the baby, he bathed her, dressed her, changed her and cared for her. He was a normal, loving father.'

Those who loved Duffy: Above - Carol Holmstrom and her son Peter with Duffy's daughters Sammy Jo and Michelle.

Right - Mother Brenda and girlfriend Lisa Stockell

"I'm so sorry that Katie Leigh will never know her father – but I will remember the love he gave us."

Lisa, 23, refuses to believe the stories of Lee's drug-dealing and violence.

"If he was a drug dealer, how come he had no house or car or money?"

Duffy had £60 on him when he died – every penny he owned.

Lee, the loving father

THE DAY THEY BURIED LEE PAUL DUFFY..

MEDIA SPOTLIGHT: Lee Duffy, left, who died in 1991 and mum Brenda, right

But if it has to be written, I would like to see something good about him, something that is fair because his kids will read it.

"Lee was a lovely, lovely boy and a lot of people remember him that way."

Hundreds gather in street

By HELEN LOGAN

THE funeral of Lee Duffy took place on Teesside today.

The 26-year-old was stabbed outside Middlesbrough's Afro-West Indian Centre in Marton Road two weeks ago.

Scores of relatives and friends gathered at Mr Duffy's bungalow home in Durham Road, Eston, before the funeral cortege left.

Two lorries were needed to carry the large number of floral tributes which included ones in the shape of a boxing glove and a boxing ring.

Others were designed in hearts and crosses, and also the words Kid No 1 and Dad and The Duffer were spelled out in flowers.

Police stood at points along the route taken by the cortege to St John's Church, South Bank.

The funeral party brought traffic in the area to a standstill. Hundreds of people lined along Normanby Road to pay their last respects to the former boxer.

Police were present at the service followed by burial at Eston cemetery.

The former boxer and nightclub bouncer had previously survived three alleged attempts on his life in which he was shot twice and had petrol poured over him.

Mr Duffy, whose parents Brenda and Lawrence live in Kit Hardie Close, South Bank, was driven to Middlesbrough General Hospital by a passerby following the last assault, with what police described as "sharp instrument". He died half an hour later.

Mr Duffy shared his Durham Road home with his girlfriend Lisa Stockill, mother of his six...

● Turn to Page 3

● Lee Duffy

● Pall-bearers take Lee Duffy's coffin to the waiting hearse outside his girlfriend's home in Durham Road, Eston. Picture: DOUG MOODY

Above: How Lee's funeral was reported
Top right: An excerpt from an interview with Lee's mam Brenda
Above right: Brian with Terry Dicko at Lee's grave in October 2020

Stephen Sayers carries Lee's coffin

Saturday 7th March 2020, Mr and Mrs Cockerill

Above: After the baptism with Tony, Carl and Emma

Above: Kev and Richard Kilty

Left: Born again Brian with Tony Grainge and Emma

Brian in training recently

A couple of days later he called to ask if he could buy some coke. I told him to come over and I would sort it out for him. My mind was set. I was going to 'tax' him for every penny. I got a couple of my mates involved from Hartlepool to act as the dealers. They spoke to him on the phone and made out that they had a big bag of coke and they told Craig it would be ten grand to buy it. The following day he turned up in the Cosworth to meet my mates and was wearing a coat that Lee Duffy had given him. He walked in oozing arrogance and knocked up a line and offered me one. I declined. I was working out how I was going to knock him out. We chatted a little and he ordered a pizza as we waited. I waited till his last supper arrived before I asked him why he had told 'Karad' that he could fight me and Lee and that we were his 'soldiers.' The colour drained from his face, "I've said nowt Bri," he said as he tried to get to the door, but before he got to it I slapped him dislocating my thumb in the process. I grabbed him and slapped him again and told him to give me the money that he had brought for the coke. He didn't have any. The slink only had a tenner on him. He had thought that he could get the coke on tick and would have probably tried to pull a fast one with that too. I told him to take Lee's coat off because he wasn't fit to wear it. I then slapped him again and told him to take his gear off. In his panic he started removing his trousers so I told him to put them back on and that I was robbing him not raping him! I took his car keys off him and booted him out of my house.

More stories started to emerge about Craig. He had got a ten grand watch of my mate 'Chino' and hadn't paid him for it. So I headed to Harrogate, which is where he was living in a guest house with another lad who was in the RAF. Bam Bam, Paddy Watson, and Flea came with me in the Cosworth. When we arrived his girlfriend Rachel saw me out of the window and started shouting to Craig that I was outside. Instead of coming outside and dealing with the situation man to man he picked up his phone and he called the police, so we had to get back in the car and drive off. He accused me of stealing the Cosworth and reported me for turning up at his door. I decided to head back to Bradford to speak to Karad instead who was only too happy to help me out. I explained what Craig had done so he gave me the Porsche 928 and said that he would tell Craig that he had sold it to me.

For a few months after that Craig was telling anyone that would listen that he was going to fight me which was laughable. I knew, at some point I would bump into him. Sure enough he was at a garage in Hartlepool when I pulled in. I walked straight over to his car and told him to get out. He took one look at me and revved his engine and screeched off. I heard nothing from him for over a year and then out of the blue I got a call from him to say that he hadn't been saying anything about me and that he wanted no trouble. I listened to what he had to say and then told him that he better just keep his mouth shut.

A month or so later I got another call from a friend in Hartlepool to tell me that Craig had died. He had got up to go to the toilet in the middle of the night in his caravan in Hartlepool and had a massive heart attack and collapsed and died. The combination of steroids, cocaine and crack had finally become too much for his body and he joined an ever growing list of my former friends and associates in the cemetery.

Memories

The stories in the next part of this book are from those who knew and loved Lee. Some people have asked to remain anonymous.

Memories: Anonymous

I first met Lee when Denis Lowe and myself had this space invader shop in Southbank. Lee was fourteen or fifteen at the time. He was doing a bit of boxing with Grangetown boys at the time. He used to regularly nick off school and come to the space invader place which was just coming into its own by then. Denis was bang into his boxing so we used to do a bit of sparring out the back. We had a bag up, pads, mitts and a few weights in there. Lee got wind of it and he used to be in and out all the time.

I remember his mother Brenda coming in one day and she said "Is that bastard of mine in here?" Brenda was a typical Southbanker. She just told you how it was but she was a great lady. Anyway I will never forget it, I just looked and there was a split door with a hatch were you would give bits of change out and I noticed Lee hiding behind the door. I just looked around and said, "I can't see him Brenda." It wasn't too long after that he went to Low Newton for a spell behind bars.

The story about how Lee got his first door job is one of my favourites. Lee jogged from Southbank to 'Le Roches' on Newport road down where the old fruit warehouse used to be and Lee asked Don Le Roche if he had any doorman jobs going. Don told him he didn't and told him to come back when he was a bit older. Lee had his jacket, trousers and shirt in a suit bag and he had jogged down in his trainers shorts and t-shirt. Undeterred Lee said, "Who's your best doorman in here?" It was a lad called 'Spanny' at the time. Lee continued, "I will fight your best doorman out here. Can I take his job if I beat him?" All the doorman were laughing at him and agreed at this kid who they thought was about to learn a valuable life lesson. The fight lasted about eight seconds and Lee got his first door job. Each night he worked there he would jog from Southbank to work in 'Boro and jog back again. He was super fit in those days.

Lee loved a fight and would often fight for big money. Lee had not long been out after another spell in jail. I was working on the door of a pub in 'Boro on a Saturday afternoon with another lad called McKenna. On the top of the pub there was a carpark that you could access round the back which was at the back of one of the big stores. You could drive up the ramp to the top where there used to be a lift. We used to park our cars at the top and get in the lift down and it used to bring us straight to the pub door. It's JD Sports today. Lee arrived and greeted me. I said, "Fucking hell, here's a blast from the past," and we started chatting away. He started coming in and out and within a week he had a fight set up with a travelling lad from Doncaster for money. It was to take place at the carpark I have just mentioned. The fight did take place. His good friend Mark was with him on the day and he turned up with no money. I never actually saw the fight but they came down afterwards and Lee's hands were covered in marks but he had won. I asked him what he would have done if he had lost the fight. He just smiled and said I knew I wasn't going to get beat.

When the travellers had asked him where his cash was he had told them that it was safe and in his car. They believed him, not that it mattered in the end.

Lee was quite spontaneous and had no qualms about walking into places and expecting to use people's things. There was a guy called Adgi who was an indian guy who had a place on Cresent road which did video rentals on one side and on the other side he used to have an indian takeaway. He had some scales there where they used to weigh the curries and spices and they would vac pack them and seal them to sell on. Lee turned up in there one day with a rucksack and took out a load of nine ounce bars of cannabis and told Adgi to pass the scales over. Adgi obliged and Lee started weighing them off on the scales. Once he had done them all he thanked Adgi and left. Typical of Duffy, Lee always thought he was bullet proof. He would just go in and demand things.

Even in prison Lee ran the roost. I went up to Walton to see him and we took him some gear. Without a care in the world he took it out in front of the screws and then swallowed the weed in a balloon. He just looked at the screw who had seen him do it and said, "What are you going do about it?" Nothing at all. Even the screws knew not to mess with the Duffer.

I used to do a lot of off roading (which is like rally driving off road) in a 4x4 and I switched to group N rallying. So I used to go to 'Birkbecks Garage', and used to do some training on their course. This day Lee was on his toes. I can't remember why he was on his toes but he was always on his toes for something or other. He had come to see me and asked if he could tag along with me for the day. Lee wasn't the type of person you would say no to. I explained to him that I was going rally training which didn't deter him, in fact he seemed quite interested. I took him with me. We were high up in the hills in Skelton looking down on 'Boro. He didn't get involved, choosing to sit on the side and watch instead. He asked me not to tell the people there who he was so I introduced him to my mates as someone else and Lee even put on a different accent. He started chatting to the owners at one point who really took a shine to him. He came across as a totally different guy altogether. Chris and his Mam showed him all the cars in the garage and as we headed home that night he said that he had really enjoyed the day. I was pleased but still bemused that this was the same Lee Duffy that had such a fearsome reputation.

We were all in the 'Linthorpe' pub one Saturday and Lee came in. He went up to Dave Bishop and said to him, "Does your mate want to go outside with me?" He meant me! I was panicking and watched and waited for Dave's answer. " I don't know Lee, ask him." He said. Lee then turned to me, smiled and winked and walked away. He loved playing those types of mind games. I did like Lee though. There were times when Lee was on his toes and we would put him up at different people's houses and try to help him out with money or somewhere to stay so he could keep out the way. I bailed Lee out any amount of times.

My wife told me a story about the week before Lee got killed. He had come to my house and asked to see me but I wasn't in. We were mates but had a few run ins, although he had never had a pop at me. My Mrs let him in and she said that he walked into my living room and sat down on his knees and started to talk to her about me saying that he had 'got me all wrong.' To be honest Lee's behaviour was too much for me and I had started to avoid him and the places that he drank in. He had obviously realised that, as he said 'he doesn't want to be pals with me anymore.' He then began apologising for making me feel that way. It had clearly hit home with him that day. I was just a straight working lad who was his pal but I wasn't a bad lad and not involved in his type of business. If he'd ever needed me like all mates I would have been there for him. In many ways I wish I had been there that day to see him.

Lee did have a good side to him. He was a good family man. Getting involved in drugs was his downfall. When Brian teamed up with Lee it was a nightmare for everyone in the area. With Lee's unpredicatability and Brian having no fear about what was behind the doors he was kicking in each day they were dangerous and unstoppable.

The first time I met Brian Cockerill was at 'Harveys' in Darlington when we were both working on the door. I hadn't long been out and Bryan Flartey had phoned me up to give him a hand on the door as they were having a lot of trouble with the locals. I remember a particular night it all kicked off and a group of football hooligans had come to the door. There was no radio so a light used to flick to let us know there was bother. I remember flying down towards the door and Flartey was trying to get his cosh out of his pocket. Brian came running up from another door and Mark Epstein from another. Between the three of us we wiped out five or six of them and by this time Flartey had just managed to get the cosh out of his pocket.

The next time I saw Brian was at Mark's garage with his son who was a boxer. There was a punch bag and Brian nearly loosened the top veranda on the bracket because he hit it with such ferocity. I couldn't believe the power he had hit it with. I put my full weight behind the bag and Brian was throwing combinations into it and was nearly lifting me off the floor. Where I lived it was a cul-de-sac and there was a wallpaper shop on the corner. There was always loads of different vans parked out the front. I remember one day we were on about strength testing and stuff and Brian came past and heard us. Without saying a word he put his back to the back of the van and put his hands on the bumper and deadlifted the back of the van up and actually kinked the bumper. When they opened the doors up the van was full of wallpaper, which is a heavy dense weight in itself.

I remember when Brian went looking for Lee Duffy and he was hiding in a few different places after their fight. Lee had told me that he had got John Fail to hit Brian with a pils lager bottle and he said Brian just reached over and pulled him right over his shoulder as if he was a bag of feathers and threw him over. I always remember John Fail saying at the time that he'd never been so scared in all his life and John was a game lad in his day.

There was one occasion Brian was in my car when the police were looking for him. Brian was on the phone talking to someone and the sirens were going off all around us. I was in a right flap but Brian was oblivious to what was going on around us. He is that kind of man. We have spent a lot of time in each others company over the years and I class him as one of my closest friends. I am pleased he has turned his life around and has found happiness. As for Lee I hope he has found peace.

Memories: Anonymous 2

My family lived across the road from the Duffy family. We never really saw much of Lee but if we did he would either be by himself or with his good mates Neil Booth or Lee Harrison. I was 12 when I first remember seeing him. Harrison would pick Lee up in his white Golf and before he got in his car he would shout us over and would just fill our hands with loose change and say "There you go, now go and get yourselves loads of sweets."

Sometimes when we were playing football in the street Lee would come over to join in. He had two left feet though and wasn't a footballer.

Most days we would sit on the corner of Normanby road outside a house. There would be loads of us there of all ages. I remember Lee walking down the street towards us one day and pulling one of the older lads to one side. He handed him a nine bar for free. The other lads saw this and were over the moon.

I remember one day Lee coming down the street and he was wasted and he couldn't get in the house because Brenda, his mam, had gone out and he had forgotten his keys. He was banging on the doors and windows and falling all over the place. He had obviously been out all night. Next minute he snapped some fence posts off the fence and snapped them in half. He kept them in his hands and fell asleep on the green. It was as if he was trying to make a cross with them. He had been there for about two hours when a car pulled up and someone asked me how long he had been there. If my memory serves me correctly I think it was Neil Booth. I told him two hours. Boothy sat there in the car watching his mates back whilst he slept.

I remember on another occasion the police turning up and knocking at Brenda's door. Lee came straight out and the police started to back off and were telling him that he had to go with them to the station. Lee took a look at them all and told them to go away and closed the gate. The police looked at each other and then climbed back inside their cars and drove away.

Two doors away from Lee there used to be a lot of bikers. One of the lads was called 'Spenner' who was a lovely lad. We would see the bikes every Sunday come whistling down the street at eight o clock in the morning and watch them drive off into the distance. One morning I saw Lee heading towards 'Spenners' house and he looked really angry. There were six or seven bikers there and I saw Lee pointing at one of them. I walked over to have nose at what was going on. By now Lee he was in the house. He was in there for about ten minutes. When he came back out he looked a lot happier. Next thing you know the seven bikers come out of the house, all looking white as sheets, and get back on their bikes and ride off at pace. I cannot recall seeing them again.

Lee would borrow super noodles off my mam and things like that. I remember the family had a dog called 'Max' which was a big red Staffordshire bull terrier. It was Lawrie's dog but Brenda used to mind it. We had a little Jack

Russell at the time and one day Lawrie's dog got out and got a hold of our dog and started shaking it from side to side. Lee rushed out and managed to get the Staffie off with a struggle and he couldn't apologise enough.

Whenever Lee would see us in the street he would always give us money to go and get pocket fulls of sweets. That's just how he was with us. I didn't know a bad side to Lee. I heard the stories of course, but that was not the Lee I knew.

Lee's other neighbours were the Coxes and the Haslams and we all looked out for each other, it was a close knit community. I remember the day of Lee's funeral and Southbank came to a standstill. People lined the streets. Coaches were pulling up. It was mental. Every man and his dog was there. Even the kids skipped school from Southbank, Grangetown and Eston to go to Lee's funeral. To the Southbank people, his people, he was a very, very, loyal lad and everyone stuck together in those days.

Memories: Stephen Sayers

*Stephen Sayers remembers Lee living with him and Michael in a house that their Dad had bought in Newcastle in Westgate Hill Terrace in Newcastle. He lived there for a year on and off.
Lee loved the Sayers family and they loved him.*

Back in the late eighties I was in the Bay Horse pub and I got a phone call off Lee Duffy to say he was coming through to see us and have a drink with us. When he arrived he had this other lad with him who must have driven him over. We had a few drinks in the Bay Horse and then headed down to the city centre. We were at the bottom of the Bigg Market and I saw this lad grab this lass by the scruff of the neck and he was slapping her about so we went towards them. I realised that I knew the kid and I tried to have a word with him but he started being cheeky so he got a slap off us.

He started shouting and bawling and then this big fat woman came to the door and started shouting and bawling at me telling me that she was going to get me fucked! Quick as a flash I shouted back at her, "Look at the state of you, you ugly bastard, you couldn't get yourself fucked!" That didn't go down too well and she went beserk. As all this was going on Lee was talking to the little bloke from the kebab shop who also had a kebab shop in Middlesbrough and was oblivious to my ongoing argument. There was then what I can only describe as a mini stampede as she started running towards me with a herd of big lasses. I burst out laughing as I watched them come towards me thinking there's going to be a commotion here. Somebody threw a bottle which hit the kebab shop owner on the head.

Before they could get close to me I started jogging past Lee and up the Bigg Market. "Where you going?" He said. Still laughing I pointed at the oncoming women and he burst out laughing too as we raced to the top of the street. If it hadn't been for a half price sale at Pizza Hut halfway up the street which distracted the fat lasses then we would have been dead men I'm sure!

On another occasion we met up at the 'Bay Horse' again for a drink before heading into Newcastle. It was chocca in the bar and Lee was getting a lot of attention from the locals. People were blown away with his sheer size. A lot of folks were wary of him to be honest. Anyway we had a good drink and a right good laugh and that's when the phone call came through that my pal had been beaten up the night before when he was drunk. He asked if we would go through to Gateshead with him to watch his back whilst he had a straightener. He wasn't sure if he could beat the kid but was prepared to give it a shot. We agreed and we made our way to Coatsworth Road in Gateshead and then to a bar called the 'Honeysuckle.' Just after we got there a Sierra Cosworth pulls up and my pal gets out followed by the kid he is fighting who was a big lump and clearly full of steroids.

The next thing I know, bang bang and the two biggest lads were unconcious including the lad who had come for the straightener. Lee had knocked the two of them out. Another car full of his mates which had just pulled up reversed and drove off after seeing Lee make easy work of their friends. My other pal thanked Lee and we drove back to the Bay Horse and carried on partying.

In those days we used to party every night of the week. We ended up going back to mine and we crashed there for a few hours. I lived in a flat in Byker at the time. After a few hours sleep Lee asked me to take him back to 'Boro. I agreed and as we were heading down the motorway Lee pulled a cassette tape out of his pocket. There was a song on it called 'Sunshine On A Rainy Day' sung by Zoe and he wanted it blasting on the stereo. Lee loved it and he danced in the car all the way back to Middlesbrough. It was such a happy time and brings back a lot of memories and it still brings a smile to my face when I hear the record and sometimes a tear to my eye, as it was the last time that I saw Lee. When the word come on the Sunday that he had died I was absolutely devastated as were the rest of my family. He had spent that much time in Newcastle he was an adopted 'Westender.'

When the funeral was announced I hired a coach. There were over a dozen cars and loads of mini buses who made the journey to 'Boro too. There was another bus that was just full from top to bottom with wreaths. When we got towards the church I was amazed to see that the council had put out fences and crash barriers. They were wise to do so. I have never seen crowds like it for a funeral. There were men, women, kids, from every age and nationality lined up to pay their respects to the 'Duffer.' It was the closet Middlesbrough will come to having a state funeral. I was asked to carry the coffin by the family. It was an honour to be asked.

I have seen photos from that emotional day. There are some of me carrying the coffin and others from the graveside where I have my eyes closed. It was front page of the local paper under the headline, 'The Day They Buried Lee Paul Duffy.' I remember that moment very clearly. I had just seen the hole that the coffin was going to lowered into and it was something that I wasn't prepared for and didn't want to see.

We went back from there to the 'Bay Horse' and to be honest it was a very very sad atmosphere. There was about a hundred and fifty people in there. I needed to change things. So I stood up and said, "Listen up. Lee wouldn't have wanted this. He would have wanted us to be fucking happy and celebrate his life." I put two bob in the jukebox and put 'Seasons In The Sun' on (goodbye my friend it's hard to die). People listened to what I said and listened to the song and relaxed more. That night we all ended up in the 'Bizz Bar.' There was about a hundred of us. Some people came in who we were 'bogeys' with. We weren't sure if they had come in to show their respects or to cause problems. One of my pals saw what was going on so walked straight up to them and started singing in his face....Lee Duffy... Lee Duffy... Lee Duffy. Everyone else followed his lead and soon everyone in the pub was singing Lee's name. The hairs stood up on my body. People were shaking and crying and the people who had walked in didn't know what to do or where to put their faces. The chanting went on for at least five minutes. It was our way of releasing steam and celebrating Lee's life. The men who had come in decided to leave. They made the right decision. One wrong word and they may not have left the pub alive if the crowd had got a hold of them.

After Lee's death my Mam, Yvonne, got in touch with Lee's Mam Brenda and she used to invite her through to stay with her. They became very good friends. My Mam could relate to her and her situation because John and I were very similar. Lee would often mention a lad he was 'taxing' with called 'Big Bri.' He had fought this man on the street and told me that it was his toughest fight and that 'Bri' was his toughest opponent. That was some compliment from one of the best fighters I have seen.

When I first met Brian we got on like a house on fire. I had been on a bender the night before and had only had a couple of hours sleep when I had a knock on my door at about 10am. Brian had been to an all nighter too and he was with a couple of lads and had called in to see me. I was welcome of the company because I was in the bad books with my lass for being out all night. When they decided to head back to 'Boro I walked them out to the car. Brian opened his boot where he had two dumbells which were a 100 kg a piece. He took them out of the boot and started doing shoulder presses with them. You could see the car lifting when he lifted them out. He had phenomanal strength. "You're canny strong" I said to him and quick as a flash he grabbed me by the waist and lifted me up in the air. It wasn't something I really wanted after having little or no sleep and I wasn't feeling the best after an all nighter. I was 16 stone at the time and he had picked me up like a two year old child.

We ended up getting on it that day and ended up in town again that night. We did the usual pub crawl and then visited a few clubs. There was a few big lads in the last venue staring at Brian. He asked one of them what his problem was and he was a bit abrupt with him so Brian slapped him with the palm of his hand instead of punching him. The lad went flying and landed on the floor. He was sparked out and had a broken jaw for his trouble. This lad was about six foot three and eighteen stones. He was no fairy, and Brian had demolished him with a slap. People watching were starting to comment. One said "Viv Graham couldn't do that." So Brian shouted, "Go get Viv Graham and I will knock him out the same way." Needless to say Viv never turned up.

Brian and I have shared many a drunken and blurred night partying on Teesside and Tyneside and I have some fantastic memories which are priceless. The same can be said about Lee Duffy before his untimely death. These men were not friends of mine. They are brothers. I am so pleased that Brian has managed to turn his life around like me and it was an honour to be at his wedding in 2020 to the beautiful Emma. I hope that they will be very happy together.

Memories: Anonymous 3

During my spell in Durham I was inside with a lot of lads from Middlesbrough including Lee Duffy's brother Lawrie. I was on D2/D3 wing and Lawrie was opposite. Viv Graham was in there too and he ran the landing at that time and did the screws' 'dirty work' for them. Davey Glover Snr was in at that time too.

One day some of the 'Boro lads were going to court. My pad mate was one of them. Back in those days you were transported to court in a coach where you were all sat side by side. This day the screw's keys were dangling down on a big chain so my pad mate managed to slip off the master key for the handcuffs without him noticing and he swallowed it. After a day in court the lads were taken back to Durham and taken back to their cells. It was at this point the screws realised that the key was missing and they went into panic mode. Word soon got round the landing about this key and a bidding war started with one lad willing to pay £500. Despite searching high and low the screws had no joy finding the key but had a feeling that one of the lads had it so they asked 'Viv' to get the key back.

Viv walked into Lawrie's cell first and then came out moments later with a loaf of bread. I went over to see Lawrie and ask him what he had said. He said that he knew one of the 'Boro cunts' had the key and he wanted it back and then he walked out, taking a loaf of bread with him. He got the impression that he didn't want to come on too strong because he knew who Lawrie's brother was. 'Viv' wasn't as calm with other lads and was intimidating them. One of the lads couldn't cope with the threat of a hiding from the Newcastle doorman so he put a note in a box on the landing which was a way of informing on another prisoner without giving away your identity. I got back from the gym to find my cell empty and no sign of my pad mate. The screws had read the note in the box and had come and grabbed him and put him down the block. They kept feeding him down there till he eventually passed the key.

Lawrie had a visit with Lee the following day and his brother had told him what 'Viv' had done, confronting him in his cell and stealing his bread. Lee marched over to 'Viv's' table in the visiting room where he was waiting for a visit, and crouched down and put his hands on his table and looked straight at him and said, " Now then." Viv looked at him but said nothing. Other prisoners watched and waited to see who would make the first move. Then Lee got up and walked back over to see Lawrie. He had made his point. This was the beginning of their feud. 'Viv' was making himself more and more unpopular with everyone on the landing by working for the screws and getting rewarded. His door was the last one shut on a night time. He was getting larger portions of food at the hot plate and would often be seen bouncing up the stairs with baskets of fruit and pints of milk.

The screws continued to use him as an enforcer. On another occasion the 'Boro lads managed to break into the probation office through the little wooden door and steal a plug-in phone. They had found a plug-in point on the landing and were using it to make calls to their loved ones. The screws got wind of this and told 'Viv' the 'Boro cunts' had a phone and they wanted it back. Another letter appeared in the box after a threat from 'Viv' and the phone was found and returned much to the annoyance of all on the landing.

I was also in jail at the same time as Lee and Paul Sykes. There was a rumour doing the rounds on the landing that Sykes had a thing for young cons. The screws kept Sykes and Lee apart but the screws would still scare us with stories about Sykes. When the doors were unlocked we used to stick close to Lee because we felt safer. I did end up next door to 'Viv' Graham at one point. To be truthful 'Viv' was always alright with us. He was like our alarm clock because he would kick our door on a morning and say 'Morning Duffy's pals,' because he knew we were from Southbank. I was actually from the same street as Lee. I always got the impression that 'Viv' was wary of us. The fact that Lawrie was inside to seemed to stop 'Viv' causing trouble with us just incase it got back to Lee. He was definitely fearful of Lee.

'Viv' was gym orderly at that time to and I used to train with him and Kev Auer, Booler, and Davy Fields. Kev and Booler used to spar with 'Viv' and do all the bag work with him. 'Viv' loved Kev Auer who was like a little bulldog. To be honest I haven't got a bad word to say about 'Viv.' Although for a big hard man I did see him face his biggest fear inside….Mice! I have never seen a grown man as scared of the little long tails. Durham was an old Victorian jail and on a night time we used to look out the window and you could see the mice scaling the walls. I remember flicking my blanket back on a morning and I heard two thuds. I thought what's that? I jumped out of bed and it was like jumping on a coconut. It was two cockroaches and they must have been on steroids!

'Viv' might have hated us at first because of Duffy but as the months went by we all got along. We got to like him and he got to like us. I was getting released just before New Year and I was buzzing. 'Viv' waltzed into my pad and gave me a cuddle and said, "Alright kidda. You're out tomorrow. Watch how you go. You're a good kid." He then asked me if I had anything. I told him I didn't so he went to his cell and came back with a big lump of 'tac.' He said, "There you go. Enjoy your last night." I was buzzing, that was a nice thing to do. I was sad to hear about his death to be honest. I can only speak as I find and 'Viv' was a good lad.

I will finish off with a little story about the 'Duffer.' I remember a night out to our regular nightclub, which was 'Rumours.' The lads working on the door that night included Molly Jeffrays, Ducko, Chrissy Molone, Micky Jeffrays, Smithy, and Brian. This night we headed in and went to sit on the stage which was where you could usually find us. We would sit there smoking 'blow.' Every now and then the doorman would come up twisting on because we were smoking so we would hide our spliffs and put them behind our back and tell them to fuck off. So this night we were all sat there chilling and stoned and half a dozen or more army lads came walking in. They were all bouncing about on the dance floor and being a bit boisterous. They were no bother to us at all as we were too stoned to care. Then Lee walked in. It was like an old western where the piano stops before the gunfight or bar brawl, the music seemed to freeze. He wasn't impressed by these squaddies. Not one bit. So he waltzed over to the full group says a few words and then walks back. He had told them to 'get outside.' He then walks to the doorway and all the bouncers followed suit. Our stoned demeanours evaporated and we all jumped up and followed them. When we got outside and Lee was on the street, just opposite the taxi rank on the main road. He was just standing there waiting. The army lads started walking towards him laughing and goading him. When they got close Lee started throwing haymakers and each and everyone that approached him got levelled they went down like skittles. In the end there was more paramedics than taxis. It was crazy night. Lee always had a car parked up with a driver for a quick get away at 'Rumours' and that night was no exception as he passed the blue lights with a couple of grazes on his knuckles and nothing else.

Memories: Buster

I've been a taxi driver in Middlesbrough for many years. I loved Lee Duffy and I miss him a lot. I still visit his grave each week and I wanted to share some of my memories of Lee with you.

I was running 'John's Taxis' in North Ormsbey and was on the desk this day when Lee Duffy and Lee Harrison got one of my drivers outside the blues club. Tony, the driver, came on the radio and told me that he had Lee and another big lad in the car and that they had taken over the cab and were on their way to see me. Lee then came on the radio and told me who it was and said that he was coming to see me. I told him to head to the office. When they arrived Lee came in to see me and told me that he was taking me to Newcastle. I told him that I had to mind the desk but he told me to get the driver to do it. He also said that we would pick up my dog too! So after sorting out someone to man the desk we were on our way to Newcastle.

We headed to Billy Robinson's house in Gateshead. Michael Sayers was going out with Billy's daughter at the time and he was in bed at the house. Lee was always joking so he took the pitbull upstairs and put it into the bed with Michael who was dead to the world. Lee was laughing his head off.

Lee used to have a CB radio which were all the rage at the time and had been talking to a girl in Sheffield. He said that the girl loved him and asked if I would give him a lift to see her. I agreed and I took him to Hyde Park flats in Sheffield and this really overweight girl came out. I said "That must be her Lee." He took one look at her and said "Buster, fucking drive away." I decided to wind him up and wound down my window and shouted, "Come here love!" Lee was horrified. I pulled away just as she reached the motor. We laughed all the way back to 'Boro that day.

When I was in jail, Lee's Mam chucked him out of the house so Dolly, my wife, put him up in our house. I was on remand and he was having parties every night which was driving my Mrs up the wall. She asked me if I could tell him to find somewhere else to live. I told her I could, but only when I got home, so she just had to put up with his 'lively' behaviour.

When I had the taxi office everything was under Dolly's name, the cars, the insurance everything. The drivers were chucking any parking tickets away and the fines started to mount up. I was in London on some business one day when the police turned up and arrested Dolly for non payment of fines. My son called Lee up and he turned up with Boothy and gave my son £500 to pay the fines off. He never asked for that cash back. It was the kind of thing Lee did. He looked after his mates.

There was a man who had been working for me who had taken a car and twenty five Rolex watches off me. His brother worked at the 'Queens Café' in Redcar. I told Lee what had happened so he said "Let's have a run down there." We went down with a couple of other lads, Pete and Kevin. We walked into the café and I asked the man behind the counter where his brother was and where were my watches and car? The man pulled out a knife and started waving it about and it all kicked off. There was a lot of damage to the café and I got nicked. I went no comment on interview and wouldn't tell the police who was with me but they knew it was Lee and they eventually nicked him. The café owner wanted to throw the book at us because he knew that I would not let things go over the car and watches. My legal team offered him a thousand pound to settle out of court but they rejected that. His wife was trying to say in the witness box that there had been more damage to property than there actually had been. Unfortunately for her husband he let it slip that he had been involved in a post office robbery ten years ago in Birmingham and had a record, which put a different slant on things for the jury and the case collapsed and were all released.

Lee came to the office on another occasion at Christmas and spiked my drink. I was shouting, "Come in car number 40" on the radio and I only had 4 cars! I ended up going to hospital to get checked over. I was off my fucking head. Lee thought it was hilarious.

I remember another Christmas when Lee asked me if I could lend him a car. I had just bought a new Cortina. He was meeting a girl and wanted to impress her. "Can I take that?" He said pointing to my pride and joy. I said "Can't you take the Vauxhall?" But he wasn't having it and off he went. A few hours later I get a call from Lee to tell me that he has smashed the car up on the trunk road and run away. It was a write off. He arrived back at the office and handed me the keys and said, "Just tell the police that it's been nicked." So I did. Word got round what had happened and one lad was talking about grassing me and Lee for saying that the car had been nicked. Lee pulled the kid and told him that he would get a clip if he didn't keep his mouth shut. The rumours continued to fly round and I got a call from this lad's wife to say that her husband had been hurt and could I put an end to it as she didn't want him to get hurt anymore. I told her it had nothing to do with me and that I was in bed. Whoever clipped the lad had done us a favour because he kept his mouth shut.

I once took Lee and the lads down to the 'Hacienda' in Manchester. From there we went on to 'Watson's blues' in Salford which had a bit of a reputation. We got there and the black lad on the door said to Lee "You can't get in." Lee asked him why and the lad started to make various excuses. Lee wasn't having it so he banged him straight out. I was panicking. The Mancs were well known for carrying guns and I didn't want to get shot. Lee and the lads were laughing as we got back in the car. I couldn't get back to the 'Boro quick enough.

Lee is a big miss. We were very close and he would ring me each night to tell me where he was incase anybody wanted to get in touch with him. I want to thank Brian for allowing me to contribute to a book that shows the real Lee. There have been so many lies written in other books, it's nice to put the record straight.

Memories: Terry Dixon

Lee Duffy was not a monster, let's put that straight to start with. There have been too many lies written about him in other books. In one book I have seen it suggested that he used to knock his friends out. He never ever did that. For me he was just a young boisterous lad who liked to laugh and joke and fuck about.

I remember being in the 'Gosforth,' with Lee just after he had been shot in the foot. Stephen Johnson knew Lee was on edge so he winked at me. He had a disposable lighter and he threw it in the fire and it went 'BANG!' Lee shot out of his seat and was running all over the bar thinking he was getting shot at again. We were all pissing ourselves laughing. He then realised that he had been had. "I'm gonna fucking kill you's," he said and then lay stretched out on the pool table and told us to come and give him a hug. You could see the relief in his face that it had just been a lighter.

On another occasion outside the same bar, Lee knocked a wagon driver out. I asked him what had happened and he just said that the driver had been a cheeky cunt. I pointed to the wagon on the road that was causing a build up of traffic and he shrugged his shoulders and said that he would move it when he came round and he went back inside the bar.

He always used to say to me that if he ever hurt me when we were messing about then I had to get him back. On one occasion he pushed me over in the 'Maddison' and he hurt my elbow so I called him a bastard and ran at him. He was laughing at me. He knew I was game.

Me and Brian have had our ups and downs but I have got to say this. We've been friends for many years. I was introduced to him by Lee Duffy. My friend Sean Envy, had a pub in Southbank. When he was at school he used to go out with one of Lee Duffy's sisters Lorraine. Despite splitting up with Lorraine he kept in touch with the family and had heard of Lee's growing reputation. Lee would visit Sean's pub and would never cause any problems and would always be polite. Sean told me that one time he was going up Normanby Road with his Mrs and he saw a big guy, little waist and a pair of pink shorts on. He said to his lass, "Look at that daft puff," and then he shouted the same thing so the lad could hear. The lad turned around. It was Lee. Luckily he hadn't heard what Sean had said and said "Hi mate." Sean's wife looked at him shaking her head and called him a shit house under her breath.

Another friend of mine called Danny who worked as a plater was in Sean's pub with Lee. Danny was about to seven ball Lee on the pool table. Lee looked down to where the black ball was and he looked down the cue to Danny's face and said "Don't you dare." Danny wasn't sure if Lee was joking or not so he erred on the side of caution and just slightly touched the black ball with the cue ball. On the same night Lee told Danny to roll him a joint. So Danny pulled out the papers and baccy and his gear and started making one.

He said Lee was just staring at how much gear he was putting in and he felt as if Lee was staring because he wanted him to put more weed in. It was starting to unnerve Danny and he was starting to sweat until Lee burst out laughing. He would do that kind of thing all the time.

Lee loved a night out and he loved a dance. One night I was with Lee Harrison and Lee Duffy in the 'Butter Loggi' at the' Herlingshore Centre' in Eston. It was an outdoor rave. Lee Duffy had cut down jeans on and was dancing around like a giraffe with no legs. It was a sight to see. I always used to tell him to get some rhythm and he would just laugh.

One day Lee pulled up outside my house and told me to jump in his car. We were going to the 'Ship Inn' and he was racing like a lunatic in an old Granada. I told him to slow down a bit and he laughed asking me if I was scared. I told him I wasn't scared and to go faster if he wanted. So he put his foot down to torment me.

We spent many a happy night in the 'Havana' where Lee would always be in the DJ box with his good pal Lee Harrison. He would always make a fuss of me when I walked in and fling me about. I always remember when Lee used to walk in the club everyone would be dancing and they would see Lee and it would be like moses parting the sea.

Another of my mates, Richy Mcquade, was on a YTS course (Youth Training Scheme) with Lee at beechwood rugby club. Lee was off his nut and didn't stick with the scheme. Years later he bumped into Lee in the blues one night. Richy was a big lad, six foot odd, and he explained that they had met on the course all those years back. Lee remembered and shook his hand and asked him how he was doing. A few minutes later Richy told me that Lee was firing a gun and all hell broke loose. Richy just managed to get out of the way.

The 'Gosforth' pub was owned by Tommy Harrison and my mate Ginny's wife, Marie, was a barmaid. One night Tommy had knocked at the door when they were both in bed. He asked if she would mind opening up as there were some people who wanted a late session. She agreed and got ready and went to the bar and opened up. Lee turned up and he was with a big crowd of travellers. At one part of the night Lee asked Marie if she had been paid and she told him she hadn't but she would be. Lee put £200 in her hand and said to her, "Well you have now." A few hours later when Tommy came in and asked her the same question Lee butted in and said that she hadn't been so she got paid again. Add the £100 in tips she got that night and it was well worth getting out of bed for.

Lee never forgot people who did him a good turn and a few months later when Ginny and Marie were in the 'Central' pub having a night out Lee walked over to their table. He had bought them both a drink. Ginny was looking bemused and asked Marie who he was. She explained that Lee was the hardest man in 'Boro and that he had been at Tommy's pub that night. That was typical Lee.

There was a lady called Pat who had the 'Ship Inn' over the border in 'Boro. I took Lee in one night and introduced Lee to her. She had heard all about Lee and turned straight to him and said, "Any slaver off you Duffy and you're getting that." And she shook her fist at him. He smiled and promised that he would behave. I decided to wind Pat up so a little later I went to the bar and told Pat that Lee was working himself and she was straight out from behind the bar and looking for him. Of course when she found him we doing nothing wrong but she warned him again as I came up behind them laughing. They both turned to look at me and realised what I had done.

Memories: Stephen Wynn

Stephen Wynn grew up with Lee and became good friends with both him and Terry Dicko. Stephen lived in Pearl street in Southbank and went to Stapleton school with Lee.

After Lee's first sentence I saw him change. He was a lovely lad, deep down. When I hear people say he was a bully It annoys me. He was not a bully. They are only saying that because he's not here to defend himself. I knew his whole family well. I also remember how Lorna Lancaster always looked out for him. In my eyes he was a gentleman.

I remember Lee getting bullied as a kid but people under estimated him. I had a lot of respect for Lee. He is sorely missed.

Memories: Emma Cockerill

My mam died when I was very young so I left home and got in with an older crowd. I was going out on the town by the age of sixteen. I first met Brian when I was seventeen. Our friend Frankie Atherton introduced Brian and me. Brian is the same today as he was back then. Kind, caring, a beautiful person with a heart of gold. We were both quite shy so were well matched. We went on a few dates and I soon learned about Brian's reputation as the best fighter in Redcar. He was doing the doors on the pubs and clubs back then. Despite his reputation he was always a gentleman with me but it was inevitable that I would see his other side at some point.

One night Brian and I had decided to call in 'Silks' or 'Zacks' as it was known for a late drink .Brian had his tracksuit on and we went to walk in the door and a doorman said, "Sorry you can't come in like that mate." I went to turn to walk out the door and before I knew it Brian had knocked the doorman through the double doors leading into the club. Two other doormen went to intervene and they both ended up like the first one. Next thing I know we are inside the club. By now Brian was just throwing people everywhere including people that were trying to stop him. There was at least six more people on the floor. I grabbed Brian's arm and said "Let's go." It all happened so fast that it didn't quite sink in what had happened until the next day.

We went into 'Sharkeys' on Redcar sea front and a doorman who worked on the door of 'Silks' pulled up outside and walked in with his crash helmet on. He lifted the visor up and said something to the effect of, "That wouldn't have happened if I had been at work." He was obviously referring to the chaos the night before. I remember looking at Brian and everything seemed to go in slow motion. Brian slapped 'Spike' (the doorman) with the crash helmet on. It made a huge cracking noise. I just remember seeing the helmet go from side to side as if 'Spike' was shaking his head. The next thing poor 'Spike' was on the floor. I grabbed Brian's arm and we left again.

I saw Brian fight numerous times after that. To be fair, he never started any of the aggro in front of me. It would always be somebody else starting it but Brian finishing it. Brian had no fear and at the time I was proud of the fact I was going out with him. Not only did he treat me well but he had a lot of respect off people everywhere we went. We never paid to get into clubs and the like, which was a big perk of being a doorman. His friends were good to me to and the likes of Tony Stubbs and Tony Johns would always watch out for me if Brian wasn't there. There was always somebody wanting me to speak to Brian about one thing or another. If it wasn't somebody wanting a debt collected then it would be someone wanting a loan. We were both suckers for sob stories. Brian would always help someone if he could.

Brian was very fit back then to and he was constantly training. He never touched drugs back them either. I can honestly say he had the biggest legs

I'd ever seen.

As Redcar is such a small town it doesn't take long for rumours to circulate and that is how I heard about his fight with Lee Duffy. I had bumped into a lad who was actually there watching and he said to me that Brian had got the better of Lee. We met a couple of days later and he took me for some food and we spoke about it. Brian didn't have a mark on him. He had a broken finger which had happened in a previous fight. He told me that he was going to have a straightener with Lee to sort things out once and for all and was going to spend the next few days looking for him. I saw a lot of Brian at this time as he was staying at Frankie Atherton's house and he used to come to mine daily after looking for Lee. We would go to 'BIBI'S restaurant for food and then go back to my flat. I had met Lee and knew who he was and all about his reputation. I had seen him in the 'Havana' in Middlesbrough and he always seemed a polite lad. He was a lad's lad and to be honest I never really saw him out with a woman. He was always hanging around the DJ box in 'Havana' with his mate Lee Harrison. I never saw him causing trouble or kicking off with anyone apart from a night in the 'Blues' when he was with some kids from Sheffield. One of them had hit somebody but only stunned the kid so Lee said, "I'll show you how to do it," and knocked the same lad off his feet and he was unconcious before he hit the floor. Lee was off his head that night, definitely on drugs. The whole place was on edge and I didn't stay long after that.

There was no doubt in my mind that if Brian caught up with Lee for a straightener that Brian would come out on top. He did see him in Eston over those next few weeks in Craig Howard's car and had dived onto the bonnet but Craig managed to shake him off and drive off. Lee was arrested soon after that but on his release rang Brian who was at pub called the 'Kings Head,' and asked him if he would meet him to talk things over at his Mam's house. Brian was wary at first but when he came back and told me that they had shook hands and decided to work together I was relieved.

Brian and Lee ran everything in Cleveland after that and never a week went by without someone telling me a story about what they and been getting up to. All good things come to an end though and Brian was arrested and then remanded after a doorman had put in a statement about him over something. Whilst Brian was inside Lee's life was about to come to an abrupt end.

The night he died I'd seen him in the 'Havana' and he didn't seem himself. He was usually on something when I saw him but this night he was really drunk and wasn't too steady on his feet. He was with another lad to who was asleep in a chair. I decided to have an early night that night and didn't go to the blues. The next day I woke up to the news that Lee had died. It really shocked me and as I spoke to different people the reality sunk in. Rumours were flying around and people were saying that taxis were refusing to stop to take Lee to hospital. The family were devastated. It was the end of an era and the funeral went down in history as the biggest Teesside has ever seen. I honestly believe had Brian been with Lee that night that he would still be alive today, but fate chose a different path for Lee.

The family have had to deal with the grief that Lee's death brought them and with books and documentaries being produced without their permission, painting Lee as some kind of monster. They have also had people vandalise Lee's grave which is a disgusting act perpetrated by cowards. One of those responsible has since taken his own life.

If the police ever came for Brian they would always send big numbers. On one occasion there had been a raid at Frankie's house and Brian's foot and leg had come through the ceiling in the struggle. One night he had been fighting in Redcar and was arrested and I got a call asking me to take Brian some clothes as he was going to court the next day. I remember running about trying to get clothes to fit him which was a nightmare. I managed to get some sorted and I then went to KFC and got him some food. Back in those days you could take food into people who were in custody. I was able to pass it threw the metal gate at the end of the cells. He was buzzing because the meals they were giving him at the station weren't enough for him. Brian and I kept in touch while he was in jail and I wrote to him a lot to keep his spirits up. I was in 'Havana' one night with a lad who I had known for years when he suddenly did a runner. I turned and saw Brian coming towards me. He hadn't told me that he was getting released as he wanted to surprise me. I was made up to see him. We eventually drifted apart and I moved away from the area.

Thirty years later Brian sent me a friend request on Facebook. He wasn't sure it was me as he had been told by somebody when he was in jail that I had died. So to test me he asked me some questions that only I would know the answers to. Once he knew I was who I said I was we arranged to meet up again. It was the best thing I have ever done and it's like we have never been apart. After a whirlwind romance we were engaged in a month and married within four months.

I had become a born again Christian four years earlier and Brain wanted to do the same. So myself, Tony Grainge and Carl Vallily baptised Brian in the North Sea a couple of months later. It was such a happy day.

I truly believe Brian is my soulmate and God put us back together at the right time. We now enjoy helping people who contact Brian's pages and I feel so proud of him overcoming his addictions. He truly is remarkable and I believe with the help of Jesus we are going to help many people.

Memories: Ian Paul Manual (Manyock)

If you were drinking in pubs in the late 80's early 90's and it went dark then it would not have been a power cut, it would have been Brian Cockerill, blocking out the sun light as he entered the building. A giant of a man with legs big enough to kick start a jumbo jet. His reputation came before him and if he was looking for you then hell wouldn't be far behind him.

A story I recall was when Brian and two mates, one of them being an old mate of mine Mark 'Speedy' Hornsby, were out looking for one of the Stockton 'Wrecking Crew' in 'The Highland Lad' pub. This story was passed on to me by Ian 'Cush' Lawson a close friend who sadly passed away but is fondly remembered. 'Cush' was sat in the pub when Brian and company barged in and demanded to know the whereabouts of a lad called 'Smiggy.' 'Cush' said he didn't know, but then a gun was forced into his mouth cutting his lip causing it to bleed. One of the lads was screaming at him to tell them where 'Smiggy' was but everybody remained silent. Realising that they were getting nowhere they walked back out but vowing to return. A few minutes later oblivious to what had just happened 'Smiggy', who was living upstairs in the pub came downstairs to order a pint. He had just used one of his nine lives!

I have got to know Brian well over the years. He is a colossal man with a heart to match and a wicked sense of humour and always has a quick one liner. To go from being a young kid who suffered severe bullying to the man he has become today is truly inspirational. A story of determination courage and strength and he is living proof that every mountain can be climbed and that no road is too long. Along with his amazing wife Emma he has reached a part of his life full of contentment and is now using his colourful past to highlight the errors of his ways to the younger generation so that they can see the dangers of the criminal world that is portrayed as being so glamourous by the media.

Brian has already set wheels in motion by talking in prisons and schools about the perils of the world he once ruled and has already talked people full of despair out of suicidal thoughts and given them hope to face a brighter future, which in itself is a purpose second to none. I would like to wish Brian and Emma all the luck in the world and may they find success and happiness in everything they do and life blesses them with.

Memories: Peter Robinson

I used to knock about with Lee as a youngster along with Brian Banks. We were always hanging around with Lee and his Uncle Rod and we also spent time with Lorna Lancaster who looked after Lee and Marty Turner at the boxing gym who Lee had a lot of respect for. As we grew older our friendship never wavered.

When Lee first went to jail I would visit him and would write to him each week. When he wrote back to me his letters were always long and he had very neat handwriting. When he was released I would always try to help him get back on his feet and on one occasion managed to get him a job so he could get some money in his pocket. I knew Lee had a reputation but it didn't concern me at all.

I remember one day picking him up in Southbank and driving to Normanby, which is only a couple of minutes drive away. We both walked into a pub there and I just remember everyone going quiet like an old western. We ordered a drink and went to sit down. I asked Lee if he enjoyed living his life like that. He just turned to me and laughed. I used to tell him he was an accident waiting to happen. After a quick pint, Lee's Uncle Rodney came and picked us up and took us to Great Ayton. I was in the back of the car with Lee as we headed up Flatts Lane when Lee pulled a gun out and put it to the back of his Uncle's ear who was driving. I have to admit I was stunned at first and said, "What are you doing you mad bastard?" Rod though wasn't fazed at all as he knew what Lee was like and he just burst out laughing and Lee put the gun away.

When we arrived in Great Ayton we went to a place called the 'Tile Sheds' and as soon as we walked in, the pub cleared and we ended up standing there on our own like lemons. Lee certainly knew how to clear a pub! After another quick drink in there we headed back to Southbank and to the 'Cleveland Pub' which was run by our mate 'Stampy,' who was always good for a lock in after hours. When we got there all the doors were shut so we went round the back. I was banging on the back door but nobody was answering. Next thing Lee said "This is how you do it Robbo" and he kicked the double doors which flew open and were nearly hanging off their hinges. We all burst out laughing as 'Stampy' came out and was flapping like hell. "What have you done? The police will come now!" He was right so we needed a plan B. I suggested to the lads that we get another mate Barry to open his pub 'Just Jives.' They said that was a good shout so I headed to Barry's house on Beverley Road. He was having his Sunday dinner. I told him what had happened and what were after and we was only too happy to oblige. All the main lads started heading down to the pub and an hour later it was jumping. Peter Hoe was there and Micky Mallon amongst others. It was a great session and everybody was in good spirits. Lee and Peter started taking their tops off and were comparing muscles and were seeing whose legs were the biggest. It was a right frisk.

On another occasion me, Lee, Tommy and Lee Harrison, Peter Clark, and Jackie Parsons, all went to the 'Prince Harry', in Southbank. John Green had it at the time. Once in there we were all carrying on, and joking around as per usual. Anyway Peter Clark put his hands up pretending to fight me so I put mine up and Lee pushed one of my arms forward from behind and it ended up hitting Peter Clark, on the nose and there was blood all over. There was no malice or overreaction though. We all just laughed.

There was a lot of laughter with Lee and that is something that seems to have been forgotten about him in other books. Another thing I will also say about Lee is that he was always well behaved when with me and always had respect. He was a man's man.

Lee, and Mark, had gone to Tommy Harrisons one day. Tommy had a pit bull that loved me and it used to sit on my knee. The dog didn't really like many other people. On this day the dog ran in and lunged at Mark and latched onto his chest and it wouldn't let go. Mark was dripping blood all over as he tried to break free but the dog had locked on now so Lee had to punch the dog to get it to release its grip, which it did. It was a vicious thing. Two days later an accountant went to Tommy's and the dog took a chunk out of his arse and leg, and poor 'Stampy' had his backside and calf bitten too. I was one of the lucky ones!

I also remember the day Lee fought Brian. Neil Booth came bouncing in the house saying that Lee had a go with a 'Scotch' bloke meaning, Scotch Bri. He said Lee walloped him but he couldn't put this bloke away. When I saw Lee later that day Lee said that Brian was the toughest man he had ever fought and that he had freakish power.

Aswell as drinking with Lee I would often train with him to at the local boxing gym. Lee was a clinical puncher. When he was at the gym he just trained on the bags and pads he wasn't one for sparring. He could have been a really good pro-boxer but he never took the training seriously and didn't bother getting his medicals or license. Lee was erratic and definitely a loose cannon. He could have been a world beater.

Lee and Brian were two completely different characters. Brian was more of a listener and was always there to back me up. When they teamed up they were unbeatable. There will never be another combination like Brian Cockerill and Lee Duffy.

We used to spend a lot of time at Aunty Vi's house in North Ormesby. Vi had brought Tommy up and I was there one day with Tommy when Lee Harrison and Lee Duffy came barging in all excitable. Lee Duffy said, "I've just done 'Jonka' outside the 'Monk," which was a pub in North Ormesby. I turned to Lee and said, "Well that's fucking clever isn't it," as 'Jonka' was a really good friend of mine. Duffy's knuckles were bleeding and I told him that I hoped he had hepititus. I wasn't happy at all. Duffy started panicking about the hepititus so I took him in the kitchen and bathed his hands in the sink under the tap before giving him another piece of my mind and leaving with Tommy. There's not many people who could of got away with speaking to Lee like that but I could as I had known him for years and he always respected me.

On another occasion Lee turned up at my house with Craig Howard. It wasn't long after Lee had been shot in the foot. He had a sawn off shotgun with him. He had his foot hanging out of the car window. I asked him what he was doing with the gun and he said he was going to 'Easterside' to sort some trouble out. So I offered to go with him but he thanked me and said that he was going to sort it himself. I advised him not to take the gun, but he just said, "They are gonna get it," as Craig revved the engine and pulled away. I saw him a few days later and asked if him he had got them sorted and he just smiled and said "Oh yes."

One bit of work I did do with Lee was with bloke who was having an affair with one of Lee Harrison's Mam's mates. I went along to the 'Princess Alice' pub where this bloke used to drink with Lee Duffy, and Harrison. We spotted the lad at the bar and we grabbed a hold of him and bundled him into the boot of our car outside. We then drove him to meet the husband of the wife who had been having an affair. They had words and then he was warned by us and we made him walk home. The bloke wasn't physically hurt just scared into ending the affair.

No matter when I phoned Brian he would be there for me at the drop of a hat. Even if I had caused the problem Brian would be there to sort it and we are still great friends to this day. I had an issue with a well know family from Grove Hill on one occasion and they had sent a kid down to do my windows with a shotgun. I called Brian and told him what had happened and he was straight over no questions asked. He arrived with a couple of other lads and we phoned the pub that the family drank in to make sure they were in and we told them we were on our way to sort them out. Moments later they were back on the phone asking us not to and that they would leave things now. I never had any trouble again from them. Sometimes the very threat of Brian was enough.

One thing I will say about Brian is that his hand speed was incredible for his size. You would think he was a middle weight not a heavy weight because he could box for fun. I have many memories of Brian. One day Brian and Tony Johns aka 'Gonz'had been to an all nighter. Brian had a bottle of Bacardi in his hand. 'Speedy' came to pick us up in a Red Cosworth. I decided to drive and we went to the 'Brunton Arms.' All the 'Park End Crew' were there and they were all sat outside and there was at least forty of them. We walked into the pub to get the drinks and while we were at the bar we heard loads of car tyres screeching outside. It was a hot day so we headed outside to see if we could get a seat and we needn't have worried. Having seen us come in the 'Crew' had decided to leave their drinks and move elsewhere and that's what all the noise had been. We hadn't gone down there looking for trouble but just the sight of us all walking in with Big Brian could be an intimidating sight for anybody.

Memories: Frankie 'Bam' Bointon

    I remember the first time I met Brian. I was with my mate Cookie parked outside 'Jumping Jacks' as we were going to the 'Theatre Club' in Middlesbrough'. We got out of the car and Cookie told me he could see Brian. I just remember seeing about 150 people outside and Brian stood out in a crowd because he was massive. Cookie introduced us both and first impressions count and Brian was an absolute Gentleman. After that initial meeting I would see Brian more regularly and would usually see him with Lee Duffy.

    Brian probably did more with Lee in a few months than most people would do in a life time. They could both fight and feared nobody. One night stands out with regards to Brian.

    I had gone in the 'Old Mint pub' with Brian, where Frankie 'Cookie' and Jimmy 'White Socks' worked in Middlesbrough and we were all having a bit fun as usual. We then went to 'Blaises' which was a club round the corner. There was a lad in there called Mickey Salter from Brambles Park. His brother was Paul Salter, one of the best fighters to come out of 'Boro. Mickey came over and started having a go at Brian so he nutted him and then hit him with lightening speed with a left hook, snapping his cheekbone which went through his nose and came out near his eye. Unsurprisingly he ended up in hospital. He was knifed to death a couple of months later in a totally unrelated incident.

    Both Lee and Brian had a good sense of humour and were very generous at times. We were at the blues on Kensington road one night and Lee had a leather jacket on that he that he had taxed off someone which was worth about £700. I told him that I liked the look of it so he just took it off and gave it to me.

    I was shocked and saddened when I heard the news of his death. Nobody deserves to die like that. My thoughts are with his family and I hope he rests in peace.

Memories: Kevin Brown

In 1984 I was told by a friend that my wife at the time, Christine, was seeing a nightclub bouncer behind my back. I didn't know which club and I didn't know the bouncer. The name given to me was Lee Duffy, so I confronted my wife over this she told me it was rubbish. I believed her and that was the end of it as far as I was concerned. I was then sentenced to three months imprisonment for a driving offence. Whilst in prison a relative of my wife, the late John Macpartland (also known as Mac) informed me that the affair was still going on and Mac said he felt I needed to know as we had three young children.

On the day of my discharge from Durham prison, Mac came to pick me up with my wife's brother and on the return journey to Middlesbrough Mac said he would accompany me back to my house as Lee Duffy was staying at my house with my wife. Mac at the time had a reputation in Middlesbrough for being a hard man. He said "If he's there Kevin I'm going to give him a hiding."

We arrived and he told me and the wife's brother to stay in the car Mac went into the house but Duffy had already left. I went in and confronted my wife and we started arguing so both Mac and her brother left us to get on with it. The kids were crying whilst my wife totally denied it again and me been the fool believed her again. I then did what everyone does when you leave prison and got in the bath to get rid of the smell. Whilst in the bath I heard a almighty crash. I had no idea what it was till a police officer stuck his head through the bathroom door and told me, I was under arrest for aggravated G.B.H and Robbery. I protested my innocence, but they did not want to know. We had to get someone to look after the kids as both me and the wife were taken to the police station.

I asked to speak to the custody sergeant and explained for the past eight weeks I had been in Durham and had just been released that morning. About an hour later he returned to my cell apologised and I was released. I asked him what my wife was alleged to have done. The officer told me that my wife along with her friend Julie, who lived in our street and Lee Duffy had assaulted and robbed an American oil construction worker next to the 'Dragonara Hotel' in the early hours of the morning. He explained that they had Julie in custody and were seeking the whereabouts of Lee Duffy. They then told me that they were taking me home and were going to do a forensic search of my property. The American oil worker that had been robbed was on a life support machine and had suffered severe head injuries.

On returning to my home they found a saucepan in my garden with half burnt credit cards belonging to the victim. I asked the Police when my wife would be released as I had three young children to look after. They told me that until Lee Duffy was arrested the two females would be going nowhere. I could not believe what was going on.

Mac's wife came to see me so I asked her to look after the kids whilst I went to see my wife at the Police station . We were given permission to talk and so I asked her why she had lied about having an affair with Lee. She told me that she was originally having an affair with a waiter who worked at a restaurant on Linthorpe road in Middlesbrough. One night this man was arguing and slapping her and a lad had intervened and gave the waiter a good hiding and that was Lee Duffy. She admitted the affair had been going on before I went to prison, and as she was being honest with me for the sake of the children. She wanted me to give her a second chance. I told her it was a lot for me to digest and that I would need to sort my head out. I returned home and mulled over my options.

The next day Mac's wife came to my house and told me Mac had Duffy in their house and Lee was prepared to turn himself in so the girls could get released. I asked his wife to watch the children and I went to Mac's house. I was fuming and ready for a scrap as I had no idea who this Lee Duffy was at the time.

When I entered Mac's house Lee Duffy was sat on the sofa. I went to go for him but Mac threw me in a chair and told me to shut up. I didn't argue with him. Mac told me Lee was prepared to hand himself in so the girls could be released and Lee turned to me and said he was sorry. He told Mac that he knew when he got locked up that he was going to get a good kicking from the police as they didn't like him. Mac told him he would sort that out and he was good as his word. Mac rang a high ranking detective and arranged with this officer to deliver Lee to him, but wanted assurances that Lee would not be touched in any way. The detective arranged to meet Mac in the carpark of the 'Marton Way' pub on Marton road Middlesbrough that day at 3.00pm.

Myself, Mac, Lee and my brother in law all set off in Mac's car, a white ex-police Ford Granada. We got to the meeting place and parked up in the car park and we sat and waited for Mac's contact to arrive. After waiting for fifteen minutes a blue unmarked Morris Marina pulled in to the car park and parked alongside Mac's car. The detective was on his own. After they greeted each other Mac told the detective that he wanted his word that Lee would not be hurt in any way and he also said that he wanted the girls released immediately. The detective said he would. With that, Lee got out of the car and turned to Mac and said thanks. He then got in the front seat next to the detective and they drove off.

We sat and waited till they had left the carpark and then we returned to Mac's house to wait. A couple of hours past and Mac rang his friend the detective to find out when the girls were being released. The detective told Mac that it was 'bad news' and that they were not coming out. On hearing this Mac went ballistic and gave the detective a right roasting. We could hear the detective pleading with Mac to calm down. Mac was saying to him "You gave me your word." The detective said it was out of his hands due to the victim being on a life support machine in a critical condition. The detective did tell Mac he would arrange a special visit for him and me so we could go and see my wife. We attended the Police Station together on Dunning Road, Middlesbrough at about 9.30pm.

I was expecting a long wait but once Mac told the desk sergeant he was there to see my wife the same detective came straight through and took us to the cells. I thought it was strange at the time the way we were being treated but I was more interested in seeing my wife. We waited at the bars at the end of the cell corridor and my wife was let out of her cell to see us. Mac asked her if she was okay and my wife said she was being well treated. Mac then ordered her a takeaway as the food in the cells left a lot to be desired. We sat with her for an hour and as she ate her food Mac told her to keep her mouth shut and say nothing because Lee was going to take the blame for the incident. This cheered my wife up and she looked a lot happier as we left.

I was still on my own with three young children to look after and was finding it difficult. I was visited by a young seventeen year old girl. She introduced herself and told me she was Lee's sister and that she had heard about what had happened and wanted to know if I was ok? It was quite clear to her that I was not okay. As we were talking my youngest son who was seven months old was crying for a bottle and my little girl aged eighteen months was screaming. My other son aged two and a half was running all over the place and getting into everything. "Would you like me to help?" she said.

Lee's sister was a Godsend. She came over every day to help me with the children and cooked me some meals. Had it not been for her I fear that they would have been taken off me and put into care and I want to use this opportunity to thank her.

Things did not improve for my wife. Her and her friend along with Lee all got remanded to Lower Newton Remand Centre in Durham. This posed a problem for me as I had no transport and had just been released from prison for driving whilst disqualified and could not afford to be arrested for doing the same thing. I had to think of the kids. This is when Lee's mother stepped in. She knew her daughter was helping me with the children so she offered to take me to prison to visit my wife which was a big help.

We would talk a lot on the drive there and back and she would always ask me how I was coping and what my plans for the future were. On one visit I told her that me and my wife had been talking and that I was going to give her another chance for the children's sake. Me and my wife had been writing to each other and she had told me that she had ended the affair with Lee on more than one occasion.

That day as we came off a visit Lee's mam was fuming. I asked her what was the matter and she told me that my wife was 'taking the piss out of me and Lee.' She then told me that Lee was not even aware my wife had three children and that he had also told her that he was going to settle down with my wife when they were released. It turned out that my wife had also been writing to Lee saying that she could not wait to settle down with him. She was taking us both for mugs and playing us off against each other. Lee's mam asked if she could have some of the letters that my wife had written to me to show Lee and that she would ask Lee for some of the ones that he had received. I agreed and handed her some to show him. This needed to be sorted out once and for all.

When his mam came off the visit that day she said that Lee was fuming and had finally seen the light. He couldn't believe what he was reading and wanted nothing more to do with her. She then handed me some of my wife's letters to Lee. I was devastated. On returning home that day I wrote my wife a letter telling her I had seen the letters she had written to Lee and I now wanted a divorce. She replied a few days later calling me all the names under the sun, but I didn't care.

When their case finally came to court they were all given three year sentences. My wife ended up in 'Askham Grange Womens Prison' in York. I do not know where her friend Julie or Lee went to. Lee's sister and mother continued to help me with the children for which I'll always be truly grateful for. Some months passed and I finally met someone else and I started seeing less of Lee's sister and mother.

In 1988 I was in 'Ramsey's blues' on Kensington Road, Middlesbrough on a night out when I saw Lee come in. By now everyone on Teesside knew who Lee Duffy was and everyone knew him as a hard man. I thought it would be best to leave. When I went to go, someone grabbed me by the arm. I turned around and it was Lee Duffy with a can in his hand. I thought, he was going to smash me up after what had gone on before he had been sent to prison. I needn't have worried as he grabbed my hand and said to me, "I'm sorry, I didn't know she had three kids and was married." I could not believe one of the hardest men on Teesside was saying sorry to me. He then asked if me and the kids were okay. I told him that we were and that I'd divorced my wife and that I had custody of the kids. He then asked me where I was going. I told him that I was going to leave as I thought he was going to give me a good hiding. He shook his head and said " You don't need to worry. I will always have your back." With that he shook my hand again and went back over to see his mates that he was with. I will never forget that meeting.

Some say Lee Duffy was a Bully. Not me. It takes a lot for a hard man to say sorry and admit when they have done wrong and I have the upmost respect for him doing that.

Memories: DJ Chalky

I was the DJ of the 'Maddison Nightclub' in Middlesbrough in 1989. I had met Lee Duffy a few times before I had started working there and we got on well. When I started working there he would often buy me my supper at the end of the night and we would have a bit of a catch up. We had a good door crew there including Paul, Dougy, Gordon Mander, Mick Willet, Keith Boyes, Butch, and Tony Trimbol who was a world champion kick boxer.

This night I had turned up late and I was doing 'Billy Pauls' downstairs. So there was 'Billy Pauls' 'Macys' and 'Maddison'. This was the night that Lee knocked the doormen out at 'Macys' in Newcastle. He came back to 'Boro and he came in the 'Maddison' wearing his white vest and blue shorts as normal. I always remember his legs which were fucking huge. He was stood at the bar. Lee didn't drink a lot. There was around ten or twelve doorman on the door. Paul Manders was a cousin of mine and like me had turned up about half an hour late. He was a big handy lad and was six foot three and weighed about seventeen and a half stone at the time. As he was walking through the bar he saw Duffy in his shorts and vest and made a beeline towards him. He tapped him on the shoulder and told him that he would have to leave as he wasn't dressed properly. There was an awkward silence as the two lads stared at each other. Then Lee said, "I will see you shortly." He then walked past him and out of the club with a big smile on his face knowing that none of the lads with the exception of Paul had the balls to confront him.

On another occasion I was on Parliament Road with Lee and I was fifteen years old. He had took me to ' One eyed Clyde Ramseys' which was a blues. There was always a big pan of curry on the go in there and an open fire. I had started DJ'ing at a young age and was working at 'Rumours' and was on twenty pound a night for playing records. Something was going on but I was oblivious to it. Lee suddenly turned around and handed me £20 which was a nights wages for me. He then told me to get myself home. I don't know what happened that night but he didn't want me to get involved.

'Rumours' was a funny set up because the DJ box faced the wall instead of the dancefloor like they do today. The Barbers owned 'Rumours,' they also owned 'The Old Mint' and 'Wickers World.' Every night when the doors got locked in 'Rumours' we always used to walk over to a pizza parlour over the road. It was a dirty minging little place but for some reason Lee liked the kebabs in there.

One night I was playing the 'Salt N' Pepper' song 'Push It' and I went to go outside for a cigarette. There was a queue of people coming up as there was two rooms one upstairs and one downstairs. Most people preferred to be upstairs but Lee Duffy was on the door with Graham O'Mally. Graham was an exceptional boxer and very well respected. Three big black lads walked up to the door from either Leeds or Birmingham and asked for Lee so they clearly didn't know what he looked like. There had been a rumour that some lads were looking for him and were going to tie him between two cars and drive off in different directions and rip him apart. Anyway Lee pointed over to Graham O'Mally and said, "There's Lee Duffy over there." The lads went towards Graham and Lee closed the doors. Now the doors of rumours were massive and he locked the doors so they couldn't get out and he walked over and tapped one on the shoulder and said, "Are you looking for the Duff?" The lad said "Yeah." Bang bang bang. The three of them were knocked out. I was looking on in amazement and he gave me a wink and pointed to me.

I got to know Lee Harrison well too. He was a great MC and we used to go to the 'Havanna' a lot together. We went to the 'Empire' one night with Lee Duffy. The manager was always pleased to see us in there because he knew that there would be no trouble. Lee wouldn't drink much at all and preferred to smoke joints. He used to sit in the corner on the right hand side and smoke a joint when he was in there.

I have read a lot of stories about Lee and seen a lot of people call him a bully. He wasn't a bully. He did a lot of people good turns. For instance some bikes were stolen from a shop called 'Bobbys Cycles' and Lee made a few visits and he got them all back.

I actually had my first 'Parmo' with Lee when he took me to Europa. I had never heard of a parmo. When we walked into the place it went silent I don't know if it was respect or fear. He walked in and ordered a parmo for us both. He didn't have to pay for it. Lee never paid for anything. When we finished our food there was a girl who was drunk and had fallen all the way down the steep steps outside. Lee and his mate Boothy picked her up and helped her to a taxi and told the driver to take her home without charge.

I'm from a place called Hemlington and I knew a couple of lads called Paul and Mark from there who ran the door at 'Wickers World.' They had a Pink XR3I Cabriolet, and it got stolen by a local twocker called Gerald Faulkner. The next time I saw Lee he pulled me up about the situation and told me that he took the car off Faulkner. I'm not sure if Paul ever got that car back.

Lee came to Hemlington one night to see 'Shandy' Boyce. They were walking down Cashouse road and there was a couple of idiots burning out a car. Hemlington was the capital of Europe for TWOCS (taking without consent) at the time. Lee saw the lads and shouted at one of the lads who must have been 17, "Do you know who I am?" The kid shook his head. He said "I'm the Duff." The kid stopped what he was doing and ran off.

When Lee fought Brian he learnt a big lesson. Brian was a man mountain and too strong for him and he beat Lee that day. Fate though had brought them together. Lee made a streetwise decision to team up with Brian when he got out of prison. They were double trouble for any dealer and if they had planned things a bit better could have taken over the whole country. Lee and Brian both loved to train. I remember Lee jogging round Albert Park and he was carrying a log, which was the size of a tree. I saw him and asked him why he was carrying it. "Why not?" he said. Ask a stupid question!

I remember being in Palli Park as all my family were from there and Lee turning up to tax someone. The lad turned round and said "Do you know who I deal for?" Lee said "No" and the lad told him it was Joe Livo. Lee turned round and slapped the lad with two fingers and the lad went down like a sack of shit. Lee said, " I'm not gonna tax ya." The lad asked him why, thinking it was the threat of Joe Livo. Lee shook his head and said, "No…cause I'm gonna go and see fucking Joe Livo." Lee walked around the corner and bumped into a lad and asked him if he could borrow his car for five minutes. The lad agreed. He never saw his car again! Lee was always doing things like that. He used to get cars or borrow cars and when they ran out of petrol he would just leave them by the side of the road.

I have heard all the stories about the so called fight that never was between Lee and Viv Graham. All I will say on that is that Lee would have made easy work of Viv. He may well have been the hard man on Tyneside but he was nothing on Teesside and he would never have come down to challenge Lee when he was on his own, never mind teamed up with Brian.

Lee had a great sense of humour and one memory always makes me laugh. I was playing the song 'Three Little Birds' by Bob Marley in 'Rumours' and Lee walked up to me and tapped me on the shoulder. Now Lee, for a big powerful man, had a very light handshake. John Black had told both him and Brian not to shake or hold when shaking someone's hand as they can pull you so you can't throw a punch. "Always shake hands lightly so you can pull it away" he would say. So this night when I turned around Lee shook my hand and he said, "I like this record by Bob Marley. Do you know what Bob Marley's favourite food is?" I didn't know so I asked him what the answer was and he said, "He likes doughnuts.! We Jamin jamin." He then burst out laughing and walked off.

When Lee died I was shocked and upset like most friends on Teesside. It was a tragedy for his family who, I know he loved very much.

I moved on to DJ in 'De Niros' in Middlesbrough. 'Boro had played Sunderland at home one day and I had arrived at the club early and there was no sign of the door lads the Lowe brothers and the doors were locked. As I stood outside and waited, sixty Sunderland fans walked up to the door and the leader asked me who 'Boros top boy was and could I get him down. Thinking on my feet I told them it was Brian Cockerill. The lad seemed unconcerned and was about to tell me to get him on the phone until another lad piped up "Who? Big Scotch Bri?" I told him that was exactly who I meant. The makems mumbled and grumbled and then walked off. I was going to make sure I used Brian's name more often.

Brian was very different to Lee. I never saw him lose his temper or in a bad mood. He was always smiling and had everybody's respect. I remember him coming to the 'Courtyard' one night where there was a bus that used to take people to the 'Millenium Nightclub' at Teesside Park. There was a commotion on the bus so Brian hopped on and the commotion soon stopped.

I count myself lucky to have known Lee and to know Brian. I wish Brian and Emma all the luck in the world, with this book and their life together.

Memories: Kevin Kilty

My name's Kevin Kilty and I have known Brian for thirty five years. First thing I will say about him is that he is trustworthy. Yes, he's been a criminal but he has come through that period in his life with dignity and his head held high. He's never made a statement against anyone and has never complained about any time he has spent behind bars. He is a generous man. I have seen him hand over bundles of notes to homeless people on many occasions and he has helped so many others in other ways. He hates bullies and on more than one occasion has taught a few some valuable life lessons.

Brian has always been fit and obsessed with training. When I first met him it was at the gym and he was probably about twenty three stone. I would say he was one of the strongest all rounders I had met. He was good at most body parts. There were a few of us training together at 'Bill Boyde's Gym' which Paul Epstein ran at the time, including Mark Johnson and Ali Addish. I remember one day Brian was in and training his legs and he had on the leg press in excess of two thousand pounds in weight, which was phenomenal. We were a bit wary at first as to whether Brian could lift it. We gave him a push up and his legs started to shake and then he got his rhythm and manage to get 12 repetitions knocked out. We were stunned whilst Brian just laughed at our reaction. There wasn't anyone in the world who could leg press that amount for that many reps.

One of the first time's that Bri came to my house on Springfield Road in Middlesbrough he met my son, Richard. Richard eventually went on to become a world champion sprinter. Richard looked up to Brian in a big way and said he always wanted to do something physical when he grew up. Brian always turned heads when he visited our house. Even a trip to the shops saw people opening their doors to catch a glimpse of this man mountain. He became a legend in Whinny Banks.

Looking back at the Duffy/ Cockerill fight I can remember that the night before I was arrested over an unpaid fine and taken to Southbank police station. Bernie Tomlin,(Solicitor) came at four o clock in the morning and paid my four hundred pound fine and bailed me out along with Bri who had come to pick me up. The next day we had gone and visited a friend of Brian's in Durham prison. We came away from there and headed up to Redcar to a restaurant near Station Road and me and Bri had a Parmo and Brian even had a pint of shandy. I remember at the time Brian was in excellent shape except for a broken finger on his punching hand. It was causing him a bit of distress and pain but he didn't tend to complain about things.

After food we went up to Jimmy Stubb's on Station Road. As we got out of the car I recognised from a distance a lad who I knew, John Fail, and with him was Lee Duffy, who was wearing a square checked rugby shirt. I mentioned to Brian who the lads were. He had clocked them and said that it looked as if they were going to Jimmy's house too. I advised him that it might best if we came back later so that neither party got to know each others business. Brian agreed and as we turned around and were walking away when we heard a wolf whistle. Brian stopped and turned to see if Duffy was whistling at him. I told him to ignore it, but Duffy whistled again so Brian started walking towards him. John Fail had a bottle of pils lager in his hand they were walking towards us as well.

    The adrenaline was going thinking there's maybe going to be a confrontation. I told Bri to take it easy. Lee came up to Bri and said something to him that I didn't hear. As Lee got closer Bri relaxed a little and Duffy took a swing at Bri, punching him. The punch Duffy threw was probably the hardest punch he'd ever thrown in his life. It was a good shot but Bri didn't go down. He flexed his legs into a slight half squat position to absorb the punch. Not many people would have taken that punch to be honest with you. Bri then grabbed a hold of Duffy in what we would call a UFC position these days and started top grapple with him. Bri had his hand over Duffy's neck and body and you could see Duffy feared for his safety. Lee tried to use his strength to push Bri into a doorway so Brian had a go at throwing a couple of punches and headbutts at Duffy. Bri couldn't use his main hand because of his broken finger, if he had been able to then I have no doubt that Lee would have been unconcious. Duffy was screaming for help saying "Get him off John, get him off John." John used the bottle of pils in his hand and went to hit Bri with it. I told John to leave them but he hit Bri with the bottle. Duffy broke loose and got a safe distance from Bri who had recovered from Fails attack and was squaring up to Duffy and telling him to "Come on."

    By now a big crowd had started to form. It was 5pm in the afternoon and a light night. Duffy seeing the crowd decided to goad Brian but he was keeping a safe distance. Brian was getting frustrated so he ripped up a concrete bollard that was below Redcar Clock Tower and then ran towards Duffy. When he got close to him he threw the bollard at him. If it had hit him it would have killed him. It narrowly missed.

    I shouted over to John and Lee that they should leave it and that they were better off making friends with Bri than making an enemy of him. They jumped into their car and drove off whilst me and Brian headed to see Jimmy.

    The rumours were flying around Teesside about the fight and it was common knowledge that Lee Duffy was very wary of bumping into Bri. Once Bri's hand healed he wanted to find Lee and get things sorted out. Mark Johnson agreed to drive him around to try and find him. It became a game of cat and mouse. Lee was a smart lad and made it his business to know where Bri was at all times. He would have people call him when Bri was in a pub. When Bri left the bar Lee would have had a call so he would turn up at the previous bar asking where Cockerill was and people would say "You've just missed him!" He knew this would get back to Bri and would wind him up. It also showed the locals that Lee wasn't hiding from him, but it was clear that he didn't want a round two. Bri did search the pubs where he thought Lee Duffy may be such as 'The Commercial' and 'Brambles Farm,' but he always drew a blank.

Lee did have a couple of close escapes. On one occasion Bri was with Mark on Eston main street in a Ford Sierra. Lee Duffy was with Craig Howard and Lee clocked Bri who was out of his car and running towards them. Lee was shouting at Craig to "Go" but the car stalled. Bri tried to open the doors but they were locked. Craig got the engine started so Bri jumped onto the car bonnet. The car stalled again and Bri started to get off and try the other doors. Craig got the car started again and he screeched off. Lee was eventually arrested and ended up in prison and decided to make the peace with Brian on his release. It was the right decision and their partnership flourished until Lee's untimely death.

Around this time Brian was controlling all the security and doors and everything else at the 'Eclipse' in Stockton which used to be 'Bentleys Nightclub.' I was head doorman there for a lot of years. I wasn't into the drug scene nor was I into the rave scene or that type of stuff but I knew Bri was. He used to be there on Saturdays with his lads who all used to wear t-shirt's saying 'Number One Taxman Boys.' Bri invited me up there one night and I arrived at 1am. I met another good lad there to called Dave Woodiar. Bri wouldn't have to do much at the 'Eclipse,' as he had a good door team. Most times he just needed to show his face and things would calm down.

This night a lad called 'Smiggy' who was a member of Stockton's "Wrecking Crew' was mouthing off and having a disagreement with Bri. 'Smiggy' then squared up to Bri,and Bri lamped him. I'm not sure if it was just actually with the palm of his hand but as Bri lamped him he ended up laid out against the back rests. He got taken outside and he was in a hell of a state. I went over just to check on him and he had an injury to his face that was one the most horrific injuries I've seen. He had a cut from his ear right the way down to his lip. His lip was literally up near his nostrils and the bottom part down near his jaw and you could see an inch or so of skin all the way up. You could also see his mouth his teeth and gums.

His girlfriend at the time came down screaming to me saying, "Did you see that Kev? Did you see that? There was six of them!" I explained to her what had happened and that she was mistaken. 'Smiggy' who was by now coming round was trying to put up one finger to back up my version of events. An ambulance finally arrived and 'Smiggy' was taken to hospital for treatment.

The police always thought Bri was up to something and they thought that he had millions of pounds stashed away, yet nothing could be further from the truth. He was under surveillance at all times. This day one of my mates was listening to a radio scanner and his ears pricked up when he heard Brian's name. "Police traffic control. Lima one to base we've just clocked Brian Cockerill. He's in my rear view mirror about thirty forty metres behind me in a Cosworth what should we do?"

"Base to Lima one, just carry on. Just drive and observe him. If he turns off let us know where."
Brian had now joined a dual carriageway.
"Base, Cockerill is still behind us but he's flashing us to pull over."
"Okay pull over see what he wants but lock your doors, this man could have fire arms lock your doors."
There is then a radio message from an armed response officer.
"We have pulled over. Cockerill's car has stopped and he is getting out of the car and he's knocking on the window base."
"Keep your doors locked open the window one inch."
The next voice on the scanner was Brian's.
"What the fuck are you's doing speeding? I'm not having none of this in my vicinity".
"Lima one, Cockerill's pulled us over for speeding, base."
"Oh for God's sake. Just leave him get on with it. Leave it for the night."

When my mate shared that story with us all we laughed out loud. Bri had pulled the police for speeding. When we saw him the next day he was laughing about it and said that he had only given them a warning but no ticket!

The Showcase Cinema had not long been open at Teesside Park. Brian had gone to watch a film but when he came out there was a little bit of trouble so Bri stormed over to stop it. As he was sorting the bother out he knocked into a security guard by accident who was in his fifties. The guy was a little bit shaken. Brian knew that he had collided with the guy and had felt guilty and asked me to drive over to the cinema the next day and hand him an envelope. I knew who the guy was from his description and when I saw him he explained that Bri had been a big help. I told him that Brian was sorry for bumping into him and that he had a present for him. He told him there was no need but I told him Bri insisted. It was £500. The bloke was blown away. That's just the type of bloke Brian is.

Bry Flartey really thought the world of Bri. There was a mutual respect. One of the things I have been into in the past and know quite a bit about was surveillance operations, manual and electronic surveillance including visual and listening devices. Bri knew about this and at one time he suspected there had been a tracker put on his car by Cleveland police. I was running a pub at the time called 'The Astronaut' in Billingham and he came up to see me and we had a look under his car. He was driving a Saab at the time. There was a metal block about 6 inches by 2 inches clicked into a very strong magnetic holding underneath his car. I was fairly sure it was a tracker but I wanted a second opinion from my mate in Leeds called Dave Allan. We headed down there with Bry Flartey at 10am the next day. As we were pulling away Bri clocked a suspicious mustard coloured van opposite my pub with a sixty year old man inside reading a paper. He was definitely a copper. We headed off to Leeds undeterred and we stopped off at KFC for some food. Bri was convinced that we were being followed. Flartey thought we were paranoid but it was enough to make us rethink our plans for the day. We decided to head to see another couple of my Asian mates called Shwebb and Rizzi. They lived just off Magnum Way near the red light district. As we were pulling up there we saw a patrol car pass us in the opposite direction. When we pulled into their street there was a Volvo with a man checking it's engine. Another undercover officer clocking us.

Flartey still thought we were crazy but there was no doubt in my mind that Bri had a tracker on the bottom of his car which was probably sending brief intermittent signals to Cleveland Police Crime Squad. We managed to change our meeting place with Dave to a leisure park in Leeds. Dave was there as we arrived and I introduced him to Bri. Dave got straight under his car and took the box off and took a look at it in his office. He confirmed my suspicions that it was a very sophisticated tracking device that sent out a signal every twenty seconds for a second or two, meaning that if someone were to try to use a bug detector and detect it they would only be able to detect it for one second. Dave then showed us the bug (tracker) and how it had intermittent signals coming out. We realised Bri's car had been bugged and the police were onto him in a big way. Dave then received a phone call which I have to admit I found quite strange at the time. He then made some small talk about my pub and said he would have to call up to see me at some point. He then asked us if we fancied grabbing something to eat at the Italians across the road. We agreed. Bri was never one to say no to food. When we got settled at a table Dave seemed quite nervous and Bri had noticed this too. About twenty minutes later Dave made an excuse to leave us saying that he had received an important message on his mobile. We finished our food, paid the bill and walked into the carpark and were suddenly surrounded by fifty police officers from various forces including Cleveland and Yorkshire.

There were a lot of CID in attendance to including a couple of detectives we knew, Mick Todd and Vic Shadford. As the uniformed officers shouted at us and told us to put our hands up, Shadford walked towards us swinging a telescopic cosh and pointing it at Bri. Bri laughed and told him, "I will wrap that around your fucking neck if you don't put that down."
Brian then started shouting at the people going about their business at the retail park.
"Hey you lot! You've probably heard of this. We are from Teesside, from Middlesbrough, you've heard about operation Lancet and all the bent coppers and fitting up, and stitching up people to get them sentences. I want you's to witness these police going to my car boot now." People were stopping and watching and listening. It was an unwanted audience for Shadford and Co. Brian continued.
 "You's surround my car now and go to my boot and forcifully open it or I will give you the key and make sure there is nothing illegal no drugs, no firearms, in that vehicle, none at all."
We were all arrested and taken to Leeds police station, but we weren't there

very long. They found nothing and were left with egg on their face. They claimed that they'd had a tip off. We all had our own suspicions as to had tipped them off. This tip off had resulted in six months of work by Cleveland police going down the train costing the taxpayers thousands of pounds. We headed back home and stopped off for a bargain bucket, which was Brian's idea!

When Bri first came on the scene he was known as Scotch Bri from Redcar. A good pal of mine from Falkirk called John who had been a bit of a boy back in the day and had been in and out of prison asked me if I had heard of Bri. He was the talk of Scotland after a photo was circulated of him online wearing a kilt. I told John that I did know him. He was amazed and said that he would love to meet him. I've not managed to arrange that yet but I did manage to introduce them by phone and it made John's day. It shows how respected Bri is up and down the country.

I had a similar experience on a trip to Manchester when I visited 'Better Bodies Gym' down there with my cousin Mike Flannigan who was a good body builder who had won numerous competitions. The owner of the gym was a renowned nutritionist Kerri Kays and he used to train Dorian Yates amongst others. As we were sitting talking to Kerri, Dorian walked in and was introduced to us. Mike had just been talking about Brian and how strong he was. Kerri was clearly impressed and started to recount the tale to Dorian who stopped him mid-sentence and explained that he was the talk of his gym in Birmingham too! Brian's reputation and the admiration for his strength and power had spread UK wide.

I will finish by recollections with a story which sums up the 'real' Brian Cockerill. There was a poor family who lived across from us on Hinton Avenue in Whinny Banks. A few of them were mentally ill but they were really nice people. They had kids and grandkids living with them but had very little money. They were suffering real poverty. Bri dropped me off in the car the day before Christmas and saw the family. He asked me who they were. He could see that they had very little and he felt quite sad for them. I explained who they were and their circumstances. Brian took it all in and drove off. Later that day he returned and handed me an envelope with a few hundred pounds in. He asked me to give it to my neighbours but not to tell them where it had come from. Bri drove off and I did as he asked and the family were very emotional, as you would imagine. They wanted to know who it was from.. Despite Bri asking me not to I told them it was from him. They were so thankful. If one act sums up the 'real' Brian Cockerill then this was it. I am proud to call Brian a friend. He is a very special man.

Memories: Chris 'The Stockton Strangler' Crossan

I will never forget the first time I set eyes on Big Bri. It was the summer of 1992 and I was only fourteen years old. I was sat on the top deck of the 116 bus on my way to Stockton Boyes Boxing Club. The bus went through the local council estates, Roseworth, Ragworth, and Eastbourne and it was as the bus drove through Eastbourne it had to stop because there was a Sierra Cosworth blocking the road and as I looked down I could see a man mountain sat in the drivers seat. He looked to be weighing in at around twenty two stone and he had numerous gold chains hanging around the biggest neck I had ever seen. He was counting the biggest pile of money I had ever set eyes on and back then bank notes were a lot bigger than there are today, and they were all twenties. I will never forget what I thought as I looked down at this big gorilla of a man sat in his fast car counting money and dripping in gold. I thought to myself, 'Fuck being a boxer, I want to be the best street fighter. I want to be the biggest, I want to be the strongest, and I want to make loads of money. I want to be number one.' I knew the man was Brian Cockerill because we would always hear his name on the street. He was our larger than life local legend. Our own Robin Hood who was bad to the bad and good to the good.

On one occasion some slink had tried to burgle our house when I was a kid and the same slink had also robbed a few other houses. I remember my little brother telling me when I got home that Bri had been round to the scum bags house and thrown him around the front room like a rag doll. This resulted in the burglar moving out and the burglaries stopped.

Unless you've grown up in a tough place you will never quite understand how important men like Brian were to the area, because bullying is rife and at times there is nobody to step up and help the victims. That night at the Boxing Club, I remember getting hit with some big shots and I was happy. I knew why I was training. I had a reason. I wanted the money, the fast cars all the things I knew Brian had.

Fast forward to when I was about nineteen or twenty. Brian began to guide me with all things to do with strength and diet and yes, you've guessed it, supplements. All of the help and advice Brian had given me I took onboard and I went from around sixteen stone to nineteen stone ten llbs. I was eating every ninety minutes and my strength went through the roof. Looking back I was just a young lad and Bri went out of his way to help me and I never forgot that and I never will.

I always loved going out and working out with Big Bri. We always had a laugh even when dealing with serious things. Brian is as sharp as a razor and he can make a joke out of anything. I always felt that Bri was the dad I never had......Years later when Bri went to prison on remand after being stitched up after setting about a seven foot tall ex-marine, I looked after things for him while he was away. He would have done the same for me because he's a loyal friend.

What I've noticed about Brian is that he's had friends for over thirty years and that is always sign of a good character isn't it? After knowing him for so many years I am delighted to see the way he is these days because I've never seen him so happy. He is happily married and he's helping people online daily and in person.

Brian has been there, done it and stole the t-shirt. He's a fighting man who has never ever backed down to a challenge. His past exploits and reputation carry weight and that is why he is tailor made to do what he is doing now. This is a exciting chapter in the life of Brian Cockerill, the former taxman who is now born again and living his life on a higher frequency. His story is a true story of suffering and violence and overcoming adversity and transformation.

I will finish with a quote that sums up the old version of Brian 'The Taxman; Cockerill "Women loved him, men feared him, children wanted to be him, respected by all".....God bless you my brother.

Memories: Lawrie Duffy

*Lawrie was Lee's brother and and very private person.
He set up 'Hope Northeast' along with two others to help Addicts and Alcoholics. Lawrie was a family man who had turned his own life around and those of others. He made a very public statement on public platforms which can be found on the site 'Come on Boro', Facebook, and many others.
The statement was made by Lawrie on the 20th March 2019.
Sadly Lawrie died on the 26th December 2019.*

Lee Duffy —Whole Of The Moon Book, important message!
Please share this post!
PLEASE READ FROM LAWRIE LEE'S BROTHER
My name is Lawrie Duffy and Lee was my brother. I have never been a member of Facebook and I don't own a smart phone so I am not aware or usually interested in most things that happen on social media. My partner makes me aware of some of the things that she thinks I should know even though she struggles with this because she sees how much it upsets me.
The only reason I am posting on this page is to make people aware that the family of Lee are not in anyway connected or involved with this book. After a couple of conversations that I've had with people I've met in the street recently and also things I have read, have confirmed to me that there is a perception that the book has in some way been condoned or authorised by us. This is not only untrue but the total opposite.
The fact of the matter is that I was contacted by Mr Jamie Boyle, sometime ago and I made it very clear to him that I was not remotely interested in being involved and was absolutley against the idea of him writing a book, I told him how much pain and suffering it would cause to Lee's family especially his daughters and grandchildren. All three of Lee's daughters have contacted me and have explained that they were aware that the book was going to be released and were extremely upset and feared that it would dredge up all the upset, heartache, grieving and loss they experienced living through their father's tragic and untimely death, which is of course what it went on to do. Also knowing people have publicly shared their opinions about a loved one they have lost.
Mr Boyle tried to convince me that he was a 'Crusader searching for the truth about the real Lee' How could he be?!! Lee died nearly 30yrs ago and much has been said and written about his life. Of course peoples points of view, opinions and perceptions differ vastly. Over the years people have used interviews and books as a platform to further their own agendas, much the same as with this book.We all have opinions and points of view and we are all entitled to them, however how many of us would like our source of pain and suffering to be exposed and commented on by someone we don't know again all for public consumption.

I would like to take this opportunity to thank all of those who were approached by Mr Boyle and refused. I like to believe they did this out of compassion for his family and the amount of time that has passed.

Mr Boyle said he was a Christian but did not display the compassion that he talks about in his book, when he knew that the releasing of his book (that contributed nothing new to the Lee Duffy story) would impact on Lee's daughters and family. They have all worked very hard to come to terms with their father's death and heal the emotional wounds only for it all to be opened up again for no other reason in my opinion than profit. I am now told Mr Boyle plans to release another book about Lee and even a documentary!!! What could possibly be achieved by this other than to make more money for Mr Boyle.

Being honest, sometimes negative thinking gets in and I feel very provoked by all of this and want to react. However, I have learned the hard way that ultimatley this achieves nothing. I am taking legal advice. I am a very private person and it has been very difficult for me to write this post and put it on here.

Lawrie Duffy

Memories: Carol Edwards

My name is Carol Edwards and I am the mother of Lee's two eldest daughters. This is a personal statement with regards to the treatment I and my family have endured at the hands of another 'author'. This man and his harriden wife have harrassed my family and have caused untold upset to those who have no wish to be involved in his publications. There is nothing professional or Christian about these people. They have upset so many of Lee's good friends I have lost count.

His vile podcast recently was so outrageous it had to be removed. They have repeatedly contacted members of my family, sometimes during the night when I have told them to stop. When they continued, court action had to be taken. His research, except for personal interviews and newspaper articles, is non-existent and he is printing outright lies about close family and friends without them even knowing about it until it's in print.

According to his so called extensive research Lee's grave was vandalised four times. This is simply not true and is a prime example of his sensationalist approach. His pages need taking down. Most family and friends of Lee are blocked from commenting on his pages. All negative comments are removed, which gives a false impression to those who aren't from Middlesbrough who view these pages.

They also misrepresented themselves to those who agreed to be interviewed by stating that the family were okay with it when they knew this was not true. They ignored the extensive statement issued by Lee's brother to desist for goodness sake. Mr Stu Armsrong who was involved in the first documentary withdrew after speaking to Lee's brother and being shown inboxes of the harrassment recieved by us. Stu Armstrong then issued a statement very detrimental to these people.

They have skin so thick they ignore any negativity. He really is an odious little man. As far as I'm concerned he is nothing but a jumped up junkie from Parkend, Middlesbrough with delusion's of grandeur.

I have, since Lee's death guarded our families privacy and chosen my friends wisely. Refusing to engage with any publications. Over the past few years due to the abuse recieved I felt I was forced to speak out as to what was happening. We were ignored. I was painted as spiteful and resentful, none of which were true.

Del Lovell, of Gangland/Gangster memorabillia was the first to listen to our concerns reguarding these people and refused to promote his books. Then Stu Armstrong spoke to myself and Lee's brother Lawrie and withdrew from a documentary they were involved with.

It has been a awful experience for those involved, dealing with what has happened and the invasion of privacy has been disgusting. Please understand we never wanted any of this.

Others can write what they please. We are all entitled to our opinions and views, but to show no respect and even abuse those involved because we would not cooperate is shameful.

Carol Edwards, October 2020

Memories: 'Ste' - Doorman From 'Blaises'

We had decided to go to 'Rumours on a Friday night. I hadn't been out in Middlesbrough for God knows how many years. I was with my mates Shaun and Mark. We headed upstairs despite warning about it being a bit 'clicky.' We were only in there a few minutes when a big lad came over to me and placed a bullet in my hand. I looked at it then looked at him. "I've got the gun that can fire that," he said. I looked at the bullet and said, "Well not on you because that's a rifle shell." He looked impressed. "So do you know about guns?" he asked. I was pissed so replied "The only thing I know about guns is the one in my boot." The lad looked at me blankly and walked off. The only thing I had in my boot was a sock, but he must have taken me at my word. Shaun came back from the toliet looking a bit bewildered. "Do you know who that was?" I had recognised him but I couldn't put a name to the face. Shaun explained that it was Lee Duffy and that I should give him a wide birth as he had once knocked out Shaun for asking him jokingly if he wanted to play tigs. As he was talking Lee was walking back over towards us. He gave me a bottle of Bud. I looked at him and he said, "I like you. You seem alright mate."

I had known Lee from being a kid. Lee would have been a cracking boxer if he had stuck at it but he got involved with idiots. He was a promising boxer, there was no two ways about it. When his mam was doing the B&B's where Tony Walker stayed, Lee's Uncle Rod had the B&B's on Victoria Road and Waterloo Road in Middlesbrough. Lee's mam used to be the head cook and bottle washer there. She used to do all the washing all the cooking and Lee would pop in and out. He knew all the lads that stayed there. With working away I had lost contact with him. Lee wasn't what people made him out to be and it's the same with Brian. People would use their names and bring both of them into situations which had nothing to do with them. He was a generous lad too. The kind of person who would give you his last £1 if you needed it.

I told him that I knew his Mam and his Uncle Rod. He wanted to know how I knew her and I explained that I had done a few jobs on her car for her. He laughed. I smiled and thanked him for the bottle but explained that I was in a round with my two mates and that I couldn't accept it. Shaun and Mark were saying that it was okay and they would get their own, but Lee was having none of it and walked back to the bar, bypassed the queue and helped himself to some more bottles and brought them over for us. As the night went on Lee told me that he was going to a party on the Saturday and asked me if I fancied going with him. I was heading to Holland the following day so I turned down his invite on that occasion.

When I was working in 'Blaises' and Lee came in I had no bother at all with him. He would just come in have a drink have a walk about, have a bit of craic with people and walk out. Lee was happier in 'Rumours.' He loved it down that end of the town. He reckoned 'Blaises' was full of weirdos.

I remember some arguing going on in the 'Linthorpe' pub and Lee just appeared from nowhere and stopped a load of them from kicking off. The situation had nothing to do with him but he got involved and sorted it out. I saw him do that a few times in pubs and clubs. He would walk up to the trouble makers and would say, "Ow you! Do one or calm down." He was like another emergency service in a lot of ways. He was like the police but the lads respected him.

A lot of Lee's troubles were started by some of his so called mates who would love to wind him up and watch him go without thinking about the consequences for Lee. John Black used to say the same. He was like a clockwork toy. Wind him up and watch him go.

That night in 'Rumours' was the last time I saw Lee. It was the Friday night before Lee was stabbed. I went back to Holland on the Sunday and the Police come to my Mam's after his death because people in 'Rumours' had said that me and Lee Duffy were arguing. We weren't, but you know what it's like with the rumour mongers. My mam told them I was in Holland and the company I was working for and Cleveland Police were going to come out and see me, but they phoned me instead. They told me that they had been given information that we had been arguing that weekend. I explained that we hadn't and that he even bought me a bottle of beer. Once they realised I had not been with him on the Saturday and instead had got an early night they believed my story.
It was sad to hear about his death. He was certainly taken too soon.

Memories: Tony Stubbs

Tony Stubbs is mentioned throughout this book, He's been a friend for over thirty years. If I ever needed back up Tony Stubbs would be the first person I would call. If I ever had to have a straightner with someone and could only have one person for back up Tony would be that person without a shadow of a doubt. Tony was in the gym when Peter Miller spotted me doing my first 500 lb bench press, which they still talk about today.
I have had some great times with Tony and look forward to many more.
Brian.

    I'm Tony Stubbs. I live in Redcar at the moment but I'm originally from Grangetown. I first met Brian when I was training in the Leisure Centre in Grangetown. Peter Miller was my training partner at the time. We outgrew that gym so we started going to Body Zone on Westdyke road in Redcar. Brian lived above the gym. Brian was phenominal. He was the size of a gorilla. In fact he looked a bit like a gorilla too. You would see him going to squat and he would start off with three plates either end (145kg) just as a warm up.
    To be honest he was a bit of an inspiration to me and Peter to say the least and we would often talk to Brian. Peter and myself, we were working on the door at 'Eleanor Rigbys' in Billingham at the time. From there Brian got us on the doors with him in Stockton at 'Henry Africas', 'Downtown', and 'Waterfront.' I got to know Brian pretty well. He is a total gentleman.
    Working on the doors in those days there would be a lot of incidents going on. There was one time I was working in 'Henry Africas.' I was on the balcony with Peter Miller and the dancefloor was below us and the place was chokka. A load of squaddies had come in dressed as Arabs. Me and Peter were just looking over the balcony and all of a sudden I saw two or three people getting thrown about and I thought what the fuck is going on down there. When I looked again I saw it was Brian picking these squaddies up and just swinging them about and flinging them. So me and Peter flew down there and by the time I got there I got one of the squaddies in a headlock and he just stood up and picked me up and started ragging me about. Yet Brian was ragging them about like rag dolls. We were trying to drag the squaddies out but the fire doors were locked and had a chain and padlock on them. There was about three or four of us and about ten of them and we couldn't get the doors open. Brian told us to move out the way and he kicked the chain and the padlock and everything off the fucking doors. We all ended up outside and were slipping all over the place as it had been snowing. We got them all out and after a few threats they walked off and we went back inside.
    I remember one night I was stood on the front door talking to Brian and this big bloke came walking down towards us. He looked like something out of the film 'The Wanderers.' Brian was talking away to me and all of a sudden he

went over to this man and punched him. The lad was just laid out on the floor. It turned out that the lad had been bad mouthing Brian in the past.

I also remember the first time I met Emma. It was Christmas Day and I was in Grangetown and Brian was living in Stockton at the time so he was the last person I expected to see that day in Grangetown Club. When I walked into the club there he was shouting "Now then Tone." I said, "Now then Bri," and sat down with him to have a Christmas drink with him. We had a couple of drinks when Brian jumped up and asked me to go to Redcar. I couldn't be arsed with an all day session on Christmas Day but Brian persuaded me to go with him and that is where I first met Emma.

We went for a couple of drinks and then for a drive about. Brian then dropped me at a house and told me he would be back in an hour or so. I went inside and there was a mate of Brian's there. I didn't know the guy so it was a bit awkward. Brian did come back for me as promised and then dropped me back off at home.

When I found out Brian had got with Emma at the back end of 2019 everyone was shocked but I already knew that they had something in the past. People said "You didn't see that coming, did you Tone?" but I told them I did, but it was thirty years ago!

Before Brian had the fight with Lee Duffy I had been putting my hands about a bit in Southbank. I was in my early twenties and as I said I'm a Grangetown lad and I had beat a few people up. I'm not going to mention the names. So I was in Kenny Greenups shop one day and a mate of mine called Nobby Highland, who was a family friend from when we were kids, he came up to me and told me to watch my back because Lee Duffy had been talking about me in the club. He had heard that I had been hitting a few people in Southbank and wasn't happy about it. I then heard from Paul Stanley (Stanna) who had been in 'Chasers Nightclub.' He said Duffy had gone up to him and asked who I was. 'Stanna' told him that I was a good lad but Lee had a bee in his bonnet about me and told 'Stanna' that he was sick of hearing my name.

Brian then had the fight with Lee. A member of my family had seen the fight and told me what happened. Everyone had their own version of events, but the consensus of opinion was that Brian had come out on top. I went to see Brian and told him that I would go with him if he was going to have a straightener with Lee. I had heard that Brian had been hit with a bottle by one of Lee's friends so I was only too happy to go along and make sure the next fight was a fair one.

Brian and I spent days In Southbank searching for Lee in all of his usual haunts. If there was two ways into a place then Brian would go in the front and I would go into the back incase Lee was in and tried to do a runner, but Lee was nowhere to be seen. After drawing a blank in the pubs and clubs we visited a lot of the blues parties but it was if he had vanished off the face of the earth. People were split. Some reckoned he had left the area. Others disagreed saying that he was too proud and would resurface for a fight with Brian. This game of cat and mouse went on for about six weeks before news got out that Lee had been arrested and locked up. On his release Lee was quick to make the peace with Brian and as you all know they teamed up.

I never really got to know Lee. I never really spoke to him. Maybe if Brian had introduced us then things might have been different and we would have been okay. When they started working together I didn't see as much of Brian. I was still doing the doors with my mates Peter Miller, Mark Johnson and 'Galla' in 'Boro and we went our separate ways for a while. I would hear all the stories flying around about Lee and Brian. Lee knocked five men out, and Brian knocked five men out and they taxed this amount and that amount. I would say a lot of these stories were true. I had seen both of these lads in action. As separate entities they were dangerous but working together they were untouchable.

I will finish off with this little story. We used to work on this this small ship that was called 'The Boat' in Stockton which had been turned into a nightclub. We would have to go in on a Sunday to pick up our wages. There used to be a little tug boat tied to the boat called 'The Gill.' We were always up to mischief. So me, Buster, and Brian decided to nick this boat one Sunday afternoon. Brian's car key fitted the ignition so we all jumped on it and went sailing down the river. Buster was messing about and was lying on the front of the boat as we headed towards a bridge. We could see somebody waving at us from the bridge and as we got closer we realised it was the police telling us to stop! Brian ignored their warnings and we carried on a bit further down the river before ditching the boat on the river bank and covering it in reeds and mud. We then headed back home on foot. Brian was at work that night at 'Chaplins' in Stockton and two coppers turned up and arrested him for taking the boat without consent. Fair play to Brian, like any good pirate he didn't dob his shipmates in.

I'm glad to say that Brian and I grew closer again over the years and we spend a lot of time together these days. I am delighted that he has found happiness in his life. He deserves it. He is a gentleman and I am very proud to call him my friend.

Memories: Tony Grainge

My name is Tony Grainge, and I lead Middlesbrough Lighthouse and Connect Middlesbrough. I first met Emma about four years ago when she came to Middlesbrough Lighthouse. She was nervous, never really made eye contact and was always fidgeting. We always put food on and she was to scared to go and help herself to food and drink. One of the other lads Luay would have to go and pick it up for her.

After she had being coming about eight weeks she plucked up the courage to come forward for prayer and she told us what she had been through in her life. She told us the things she was struggling with; taking drugs daily, selling drugs, gambling. A lot of things that really had a grip on her anxiety, loads of fear. So I went to lead her in a prayer of repentence so she could know she could be forgiven for doing that, but not just forgiven but set free from it as well. She also talked about some of the things that had happened to her in her past through her childhood and adult life.

Forgiveness, being the central part of the Christian faith, she forgive all those people who had hurt her and I led her through a prayer. A prayer that said sorry for the way she had been living, sorry for the people who had hurt her in the past and believing that Jesus had paid the price for her to be forgiven and to strengthen her. To live a new way by his Holy Spirit.

So we prayed and she was like, "Wow, I feel amazing!" Her friend Leanne, who was with her said to Emma "Look at your eyes, you look completely different." I believe that Emma got born again at that instant. I don't believe that it happens to every person, that they become born again instantly, but I believe Emma did. She went home and all the drugs that she had, she flushed them down the toilet. I mean, at this point she didnt leave the house without drugs. She even came to church with drugs in her bag incase she felt that she needed them. She couldnt get out of bed without taking drugs and she decided to flush them all away and thats a sign of repentance and wanting to live a new life.

At that time Emma was bringing more people to Middlesbrough Lighthouse than anyone. People could see the change in her and they wanted that in their own life. When we would go to Redcar for coffee we would be walking down the high street in Redcar you could guarentee we would pray for usually about three people. Emma was very direct. I suppose if you had been as broken as Emma had been, and you could see other people in this kind of pain and knew the answer was in Jesus and loving people, it is hard to walk past people. So we would always go and pray for people.

I remember Emma saying she didn't think she had ever been happy in her life untill she had met Jesus, and now she had and has got a proper bounce in her step and a real love for people.

Emma used to tell story's about Brian. About when she used to live in a bedsit in Redcar, but they were never like personal stories. It was more like she was there as a eyewitness when different things had happened. She always used to say he is not like what you expect, or he's not like the stories that you hear. She would say he's always had a good heart.

When she said she was going to message him she said "I'm going to reach out to him" and I was a bit puzzled. I said "Why do that?" and she said "He might need Jesus. He has been through a hard time." so I thought fair enough and then she said "I used to go out with him when we were younger."

Now people say about other people "nothing would suprise me". It can be like a turn of phrase, but I can honestly say about Emma nothing would suprise me so when she told me she used to go out with Brian it just shook me. I thought 'Why hadn't you told me this earlier?' and yeah it really did just make me laugh.

Within a couple of days of Emma meeting and getting back with Brian she wanted me to come round and meet him. We had made an agreement that I was going to give any future husband the once over. I was thinking a steady 9-5 type would be good for Emma. A solid Christian, someone who had been a Christian for years. Probably a Sunday School teacher, help calm her down a little bit. So Brian Cockerill, known for being the hardest man in Teesside, robbing drug dealers, wasn't who I had in mind!

When I met Brian I did warm to him straight away. I found him very likable, a good conversationalist and I could see why Emma liked him. I could also see the good heart that Emma had talked about. Through the conversation Brian had talked about some different injurys and I prayed with him at the end. Later on in the evening Emma sent me a video of Brian shadow boxing, saying his shoulder had been healed.

Reading Brian's first book 'The Taxman' and watching his documentry on Channel 5, I got the impression he was arrogant and full of himself and sometimes when I look at some of the Youtube comments I get the impression that some other people feel like that, but I don't see him that way now. When Brian talks about fighting he says he beat everyone that he ever fought. He did have confidence in being the hardest man in the UK and all top fighters have that confidence and they do carry that. He talks about lifting weights and squatting 800 lbs and theres videos on YouTube of him squatting 700llbs. Now, when I saw that video it didnt mean that much to me, but then I saw a interview with Arnold Schwarzenegger saying he used to squat 550 lb. So when Brian's squatting 250 lb more than Arnold Schwarzenegger it kind of puts it in context of how strong Brian was.

All top fighters and anyone whos got that mindset needs to have that self belief and confidence of what they can do. But in life I find Brian to be humble I find him to be a man who listens and asks questions when we talk about circumstances. He's not like, it must be this way or my way. He listens, not that we always see eye to eye and always agree on how to deal with things! But he always listens.

When we have our weekly Bible studies asks questions, I think Brian isn't an arrogant man. I think he's a man who is confident in his ability and I see him as a humble man.

The first time Brian came to church was in Newcastle. I remember on the drive up as we were talking, Brian said he felt a bit nervous. He explained that it felt like he was going for a fight, just that buzz, kind of adrenaline feeling. At the meeting I felt that Brian was a bit out of his comfort zone. He wasn't his usual loud, confident, bubbly self. He just sat down and observed.

In the coming weeks and months I'm not totally sure what the turning point was where he said "I want to be a Christian, I want to get baptised. I want to devote my life to God." It's a big step to get baptised, where the old person dies and the new person comes to life. That's what becoming a born again Christian is. So I spoke to Brian about it and he said he was ready and it is the life he wanted to live. So me, Carl Vallily and of course Emma went down to Redcar beach to baptise Brian. With Brian being so big I was pleased Carl was there to help us!

After we had baptised Brian we came back to the beach and Brian said "Today's the best day of my life. I've done it!" I believe that was the day Brian became born again. When he said it was the best day of his life he looked at Emma and said "I loved getting married and I loved our wedding day as well, but this is the best day of my life."

Although I said initially that Brian wouldn't have been the one I chose for Emma, based on his reputation and based on what I knew. But after getting to know Brian I'm definitely happy him and Emma are together and I do believe God brought them together. On their wedding day you could feel the magic in the air. Now, every wedding is not always like that but when Brian and Emma were saying their vows and making that commitment to each other I definitely feel that the Lord was there and joining them together. It's a spiritual thing when two become one and I believe thats what Brian and Emma are. I believe Jesus was at the wedding and I believe he's at the centre of their relationship.

I knew Emma was never going to be suited to a normal 9-5 job. What I really love about Brian and Emma is all the different ideas and entrepreneurial kind of stuff they come up with between them. I mean, obviously they've written this book together and they have got a few different ideas in the pipeline that they are working on and I do love that. I love the way they work together, the excitement and the creativity.

Brian told me the other week when he was training he felt God speaking to him about all these different ideas they could be doing and working together. I love how they are making things happen and they seek the Lord in what to do as well.

I hope that people reading this book can take a lot of hope from Brian and Emma's lives. If you look at Brian's life, it was fighting at a high level which took him to making money criminally, to the desperate lows of addiction. And Emma's story, itself wrapped up in addiction and anxiety and not wanting to leave the house. So this is a story of hope, it's a story with Jesus that shows there is a way out. I hope people reading this know that they don't have to get stuck in the same old, same old. There is more to life than this. God has created you, hes got a plan for your life. He loves you and wants you to know him. He wants you to know you can live in love, joy and peace. When you have God you have an inner strength to be able to cope with anything.

God bless you all.

Memories: Ben Spann - Change Your Life, Put Down Your Knife

My name is Ben Spann and I'm the founder of anti-knife movement campaign 'Change Your Life, Put Down Your Knife'. This campaign was started because of many reasons. Lived experiences, a mental breakdown and having a 14 year old son myself, Jacob.

Knife crime is at its highest ever recorded level. Kids are killing kids for something as simple as looking at one another in the wrong way or living in the wrong postcode. The most common reason is county lines.

At the beginning of 2020 I suffered a breakdown which resulted in me reevaluating my life. The outcome was this amazing campaign.

I've followed Brian since I watched his TV documentary on Macintyre's Underworld many years ago. His was the first gangster documentary I had ever watched. The older I got and the better the internet became it was easier for me to keep up to date with the Taxman's antics.

I knew I wanted Brian involved in the campaign because of the life he has lived. If anybody could help change the thought process of the kids it would be Brian. I attempted to get hold of him but was blocked by his agent / author at the time who was deleting all forms of contact I was trying to make. Out of the blue I received a message from Brian's wife Emma who was so helpful. I explained what we was doing and asked for their help with the campaign, which they agreed. I arranged a visit to go and see them in their home town to give them a campaign T-shirt and explain all about our campaign. I was over the moon when they both agreed to become part of our campaign team to help cover the North East area.

I cannot believe how much we have achieved in such a small amount of time. Our main social media platform is Facebook and we have had a overwhelming response. We have built up an amazing team who deal with day to day running of the campaign. Our values are Prevent, Rehabilitate and Educate. We have broke the campaign down into these sub headings to help make a positive inpact in protecting our future generations.

One avenue we are approaching with our prevention program involves sponsoring sports facilities with sports kits and equipment to help create awareness on the effects of knife crime. Our rehabilitation program involves a training centre which came into being after a young local lad lost his life tragically to knife crime, Gus Davis. The centre caters for young offenders, expelled kids or kids stuck in the system.

We have several educational programs in place which cater for junior and secondary schools and also youth facilities programs in place. One of these programs include notorious ex-criminals attending and sharing their experiences in and out of prison.

We understand that this is a very hard subject to tackle and it will not happen over night. But we will all continue chipping away and carrying out out great work.

Please follow us on social media
YouTube - Change Your Life Put Down Your Knife
Instagram - PutDownYourKnife
Facebook - Change Your Life Put Down Your Knife

Ben Spann, October 2020.

The Final Word

If you are reading this now and think 'taxing' sounds like a career option then let me tell you, as a man that knows, that it's not. Many of the people I have mentioned in this book are no longer here today. They are dead. Six feet under. They have either been murdered, killed themselves or have overdosed. There is nothing glamorous about that. Take a look in the mirror and think about the consequences of your actions and whose lives you will affect. It's never too late to change. Don't follow in mine and Lee's footsteps. Please.

Brian Cockerill 2020.

You can follow Brian on Facebook via his 'Brian Cockerill' page and the 'Taxmen Of Teesside' page. He also has a YouTube channel, where he posts regularly. These are the only social media pages Brian is associated with.

Also Available From Bad Boys Books

Operation Sayers

     Operation Sayers takes a detailed look at the notorious Sayers brothers rise to the top of the criminal ladder on the backstreets of Newcastle's West End and the authorities attempts to bring them crashing back to earth by any means necessary.

     The Sayers family were once described by 'Northumbria Police as a 'new breed of criminal.' Brought up in the West End of Newcastle by a career criminal father and a mother who was a paid up member of Mensa they were always going to rise to the top of the criminal tree.

     The book exposes corruption at the highest level, the use of drug fuelled informants, and how one member of a rival family broke the criminal code to land Stephen Sayers in court. The book also reveals for the first time the full details of 'Operation Insight' which was set up to put Stephen Sayers in jail for the rest of his life.

     Available now from www.badboysbooks.net

Also Available From Bad Boys Books

The Sayers: Tried and Tested At The Highest Level

Stephen Sayers is one of the most feared men in the country, with a reputation that's preceded him in the dozens of prisons he's served time.

The Sayers family have been known on the streets of Tyneside for decades. No one else comes close to their level and it is widely known that they 'run Newcastle'. Rumoured to be behind countless violent multi-million pound armed robberies, unsolved gangland murders, extortion rackets and organised crime in general, Stephen, his brothers and associates are an unstoppable force. They've remained tight-lipped about their exploits… until now.

Stephen earned respect at an early age, blazing his own trail and coming out on top by any means necessary. A true bad lad in every sense, he gives us a first-hand account of growing up as a Sayers and living up to the reputation that the name holds.

Available now from www.badboysbooks.net